I OWE YOU NOTHING

Victoria Robinson

I Owe You Nothing
Copyright © 2021 by Victoria Robinson

Education /Teaching/ School

Library of Congress Control Number: 2021922907
ISBN-13:   Paperback: 978-1-64749-637-1
            ePub: 978-1-64749-638-8

All rights reserved. No part of this publication may be reproduced, distributed, or transmitted in any form or by any means, including photocopying, recording, or other electronic or mechanical methods, without the prior written permission of the publisher or author, except in the case of brief quotations embodied in critical reviews and certain other noncommercial uses permitted by copyright law.

Although every precaution has been taken to verify the accuracy of the information contained herein, the author and publisher assume no responsibility for any errors or omissions. No liability is assumed for damages that may result from the use of information contained within.

Printed in the United States of America

GoToPublish LLC
1-888-337-1724
www.gotopublish.com
info@gotopublish.com

I want to take this opportunity to explain what this book is about. It is about sperm and egg donors, and real parents who may or may not take responsi bility for their actions. I am not talking about the people who attend the sperm banks or surrogate mothers or women who let people use their eggs to bring life into this world. Those people are blessing others for shortcomings, that they may have. You will see the words donor and real parent, a lot but look at the explanation first.

A sperm and egg donor, to me are men and women who have children and do not take care of the blessings that God has presented them with in their lives.

I guess they do not want to be responsible. I think that it's so trifling! I don't want to come off as snapping or ghetto fabulous, but I am furious regarding donors not being responsible.

A "real" parent is the parent that is there everyday in the daily activities of the child. The real parent is the parent who is the key factor in the child's life. The real parent takes the responsible role for the child. The real parent is also the Child's First Teacher and the positive guide in the child's life, on all levels.

The sperm and egg donor usually only care about themselves. They want to be around or only see the child(ren) when it is convenient for them. It must be nice to wake up and say: "Oh, today, I want to see my child". Real parents are blessed to see the child daily. Even when the sperm or egg donors come to see the child, they come empty handed or come when they need something from the child or real parent. They don't want to be there for the feedings, colds, illnesses immunizations, giving the child the things they need, love, support emotionally, socially, physically and spiritually); or attend events; making sure the child is taken care of; and just being there throughout the child's life. Sperm and Egg Donors tend to make empty promises(lies)to the child. Then the real parent has to pacify or accommodate the child when the donors lie.

Real parents try to do their best by not talking or saying bad things about the donors; especially when the child is in earshot. But, sometimes a real parent just ends up breaking down with anger and tears; and sometimes this does happen in front of the child; or the child will hear the parent while this breakdown is happening. The real parent wants the child to have that bond with th e donor because it's something that Ute child usually wants and needs.

However, a real parent cannot make a donor do the things that a donor is suppose to do for the child nor, should have to. The real parent often wonders if the donor realizes that the child is a blessing; and that we are all God's children; that God takes care of us, as His children; and why can't the donors get it through their heads. Donors arc there for the conception of the child but, don't want to be part of taking care and sharing the love of the child. "Guess What?" It's Their Loss!! Donors only, get to miss first steps, first words, coos, laughs, ahhs and oohs, everyday hugs, and miss the upbringing of their child because they cannot get over self first.

Sometimes, people might become a donor, later on in life. The child(ren) end up with the absent parent because the real parent who had them before may do something out of character (drugs) or whatever. I think even as a junkie you should still do for the child(ren). Maybe, then, the junkie wouldn't have the money for the drugs; and junkies with kids wouldn't exist. They need to put that energy, time and money into your child(ren). Be A Parent!

Some Sperm and Egg donors feel that if they are not with the real parent, that making the child suffer by not doing for the child is okay. "Guess

What?"—Big Lie." If the real parent doesn't want the donor they should get over it and realize a child needs love and support, everyday from both parents. It doesn't stop, it's a constant cycle! Even if children don't receive what they want, the need is definitely there. But here's the way to think of that: donors, you arc an adult! You can provide for yourself. The child is a minor and cannot provide for him/herself.

Donors should realize that someone took care of them, why can't donors take care of their own child or children? Donors, don't know who will have to pick out their nursing home or take care of them, later. That, in itself should make donors want to do right by their child(ren). To all my real parents: Kudos!

Thumbs Up! Good job! As someone told me: "It Hurts Now; But, It Will Get Greater Later!"

There are so many topics or aspects that could be talked about on donors not being responsible and real parents being responsible for a child. r will try and touch on some of these, and give some options/opinions on the subjects. Maybe, this will be an eye opener to some of the sperm/egg donors. It might also be an eye opener to real parents.

Some topics/aspects are:

1. Child Support
2. Dating
3. Sacrifices
4. Whose Really Losing Out
5. Are You A Donor or A Real Parent
6. Donor Families
7. Welfare Recipients
8. How To Become an Effective Parent If You Are A Donor
9. How Not To Become A Donor

Okay, here we go:

CHILD SUPPORT:

Child Support is a great thing for children, when it works. There are real parents that pay child support, as well as give daily or whenever a child is in need. They know that they are responsible and they take responsibility for meeting the child's wants, needs and desires. They further know that sometimes the child support check isn't enough to cover the needs. Real parents see their child(ren) often and/or interact with the child(ren). Sometimes child support does not work for these parents. They might have a child with someone who might not let them see the child, at all. I personally feel like a child should see the donor whether the donor pays support or not. Let me explain my point on this. It will help you determine if you are a real parent or a donor. Donors, make choices, whatever choice you make for the relationship to be with their child(ren), is on them. If you want your child to know you will never do anything for them then, "Guess What, "That's On You." When your child grows up hating you or not respecting you, don't get mad. "You reap what you sow." "You get back what you instill (plant) in your child(ren). It's not fair to the child. "God knows and sees all." Then as donors, most of you wonder why things are not so well in your life.

Donors tend to avoid child support, at all cost. They will work "under the table" for cash, and the child never see any of the money. You, donors are dressed fresh to death and your child doesn't have underwear, pampers, food or clothes. You want to come around dressed, riding in your car and may even call from your job, but won't pay support. Donors may go to court because they cannot get to see the child or so they won't have to pay so much. The child support check is never enough. Yes, you are absolutely correct. It is never enough.

Sometimes, we can't just blame the donors, for not being responsible. Sometimes, the system or government help contribute to the donors' irresponsibility. They let real parents sign up for support. They tell the real parent when they sign up for child support that the donor in the situation can never get help from them financially. In Minnesota, donors are not suppose to get assistance, have driver license (they are suppose to be revoked), get food stamps or get financial loans for school. It's aU a lie.

Donors sometimes take this route and the counties let them do it. Donors go into some type of rehab program (drugs, alcohol or other addictions). Then, the county will give donors assistance: cash, food stamps, clothing vouchers, medical and dental care; and the child gets nothing. But, if the child has a real parent that gets up and goes to work everyday and make money, the county tells them, "Oh, you make too much money to qualify for anything! But, the real parent is the one caring for the child, everyday: making sacrifices, prioritizing and making sure that the child(ren) has what they need.

Donors get mad and want to know where the money is going; or if the real parent is dating someone. They feel like their money is spent on that person and not the child. Let me say this:" If you are a real parent, I truly believe that if you arc dating someone, that person that you arc dating is contributing to you and your child in a positive way at least, I hope. The child support is not going to, or for the person whom you are dating. Donors should think: "that person is there with my child doing the things that I am not doing. That should make me want to also contribute to my child(ren) life and happiness in a positive way." What will eventually happen, if that other person is the positive one, guess where the respect is going, not to the donor! We will get to that a little later.

To the ones who are parents and are using the child support for other people, Guess What, "That's your child's money."! I'm not saying, don't use it to pay your bills and your financial obligations. Just make sure that you are providing for your child; that includes: rent, food, clothes, utilities, field trips, uniforms, etc. Child First! Then you can play. And yes, I know real parents that all your money goes to that, too. It's kind of a win—lose situation, sometimes. But, you never lose, if your child comes first. So, donors pay your child support and take extra care of your child. Think like this: Hopefully, I have chosen a reliable person to have a child with and that they are doing what they are suppose to do. States and counties please don't let donors get away with being irresponsible. Real parents don't get a break; why should the donor?

Don't just look at it as another case or situation; look for what is best for the child at the present time and the future.

DATING:

True enough, some things are repetitive, so you might see things in more than one topic, however, the bottom line is the child.

Every "real parent" situation is different. You could be: single and looking, you could be married or remarried, but somehow dating is or was involved. If you are a real parent, who is single, you are sometimes caught between a rock and a hard place. Your child always wants the donor(absent parent). If you are an absent parent, but doing what you are obligated to do, "Guess What?" this is not directed toward you. (Keep being positive in your child's life). The single real parents have to deal with what is best for the child and themselves. The parent has to find that right person or can opt out and just deal with self and the child.

But, if you choose to date, make sure your date is mature, nurturing, honest, kind, and available. Make sure your date has patience and can love you and your children(whether giving or receiving love). You are a package deal! Don't allow a person to come into your life who wants only you or wants only your children. Be aware of predators, abusers, and neglectors. Parents should want someone that will love their child(ren) the way, or as the parent loves them. Someone, that would at least put them on that same pedestal that you the parent put them on, or even higher. Parents shouldn't want anyone that will put them or their child(ren) in harm's way or in a negative position. Repetition: Kids First!

Donors will worry or try to make the parent feel bad because the parent is looking for companionship or dating. Tell the donor to get off your back, to give you a break and babysit (lol).

Let's see how fast that happens. Donors have no say in the parent's dating, unless there are signs of abuse. The single parent must make smart and healthy choices. The donor should not get mad, if the single parent is dating and the person they are dating is doing more for the child than the (donor) is doing. "Don't get mad, get even". I bet your child will like the attention. Don't argue in front of your child. Try to get along. This does not mean the parent has to let the donor come in or try to run the house, just because the parent is single. The donor can still come and visit the child. Just show respect. "God's watching". Let the donor know your rules: No spending the night; no, you are not eating me and my child's food, especially, when the donor doesn't care if your child eats, on a daily basis. Tell the donor to eat where they spend their money and time (Sorry, I got off track for a minute). To the real parents who are dating, married or remarried: don't let the donors mess up what you have accomplished. When the donors had the opportunity to act right and be there for the child, they did not take the opportunity or were not willing to be there for the child. Take that positive person that you are dating (I'm assuming that person is positive) and love them and your child, unconditionally. Gain all the things you want and show the children that they are in a family. As always, anything that is built on a solid foundation (God, Love, Truth and Understanding), will prosper. No weapon formed against you shall prosper and what God has blessed you with, let no Donor put asunder(paraphrased).

SACRIFICES:

Now, this topic is a hard one for me; the reason being, a real parent always puts the child's needs, first. The real parent is going to do what has to be done for the purpose and goal to take care of the child. A donor would say stupid things like: "I told you about getting the child everything he/she needs, when obviously, they haven't made a contribution for a need, want or a desire.

And if the real parent calls or contact the donor, there is always something more important going on. As real parents, one might skip or pay half of a bill that's due, and go without clothing, food, shoes, socks, underwear, gas or necessities for years.(I know a mother who went without her insulin for three weeks because of her child's needs). The parent will basically live by "robbing Peter to pay Paul," so to speak. Although, there are real single parents that have all they may need (Guess What)? Fortunately, this topic is not for you and you are an inspiration to all.

A donor will see or know that the child needs shoes, pampers, socks, food or whatever and wouldn't even care. The donor will have on the latest name brand gear, and the child will have only what the real parent can afford, whether it's a "hand-me-down" or "not name" brand gear. And then, the donor won't offer to take the child(ren) shopping or contribute to it; And lo and behold, if donors arc paying child support, they feel like it should be enough. Well, it's not! Repetition: Kids Come First! They are constantly growing, needing and wanting.

There are even more things for which parents may have to sacrifice. Parents cannot say no or don't have money for every want or need either. Sometimes, there are things like: field trips, learning tools, educational needs that the child may need; or even to attend church, after school activities or other social events, that the child may be obligated to attend. It may be a last minute notice. But, I forgot, if you are a donor, this means nothing to you!

Then, as a real parent, we hear the donor get "balls" and try to tell the parent what should have been done, instead of just saying "yes", "sure", "I got this". Donors don't even want to babysit or give the real parent a break. In addition, the donors may want to get paid for babysitting their own child. A real parent, probably pays for day care, medical, and dental bills as well and the donor doesn't see that. The real parent never gets a "thank you" or "you are doing a great job" compliment from the donor. But, let one thing happen out of the "norm," and you are called "the worst parent in the world. when "guess what," the donor wasn't there, either. Donors go around town, talking about what the real parent is not doing, instead of saying: "the real parent is doing a great job; and that the real parent took control and initiative to be a real parent, God Bless the real parent and that the donors are willing to help."

WHOSE REALLY LOSING OUT!?

Now, do I really have to ask this? Okay, for the elephant in the room, It's The Child!

Children, especially during this day and age, are so smart. They pick up on everything; whether it's good, bad, positive or negative. Then, they try to figure things out. However, they are innocent victims, through it all.

Whether they are between two homes, living with the real parent and knowing that their donor(my choice of words) does not or will not do anything for them; or the little bit that they do contribute does not help very much; and some want it back(how dumb is that). Whether it's a birthday, Holiday, mother or father's day, dances, dinners, social events or issues. Kids are the ones losing out. Repetition: It's what you instill (plant) in them. Although, sometimes they might do some things that a real parent didn't teach them (usually out of rebellion). Children should always know that they are loved, respected, and cherished at all times. They should feel that they will be raised in an unconditional, loving and positive atmosphere with two real parents that love them. Donors, get on board! You never know what or who you are raising what your child might say about you, or how you might be introduced to someone who they consider important to them. This is my sperm or egg donor: Your name here ! Don't miss out on being a positive part of your child's dreams and life because you've decided to be selfish, to be a donor instead of a real parent with a positive aspect and a positive impact on/in their lives.

ARE YOU A DONOR OR A REAL PARENT?

I'm writing this so that you can decide who you are or who you want to be in your child's life. If I step on your toes or upset you in any way, I am not apologizing. Repetition: Kids Come First! You know whether you are a donor or not, and you also know, if you are a real parent. Maybe, you are a real parent, and you are in that situation where you are doing the things that you are suppose to do and not getting the reaction and respect you want from the donor. All I Can Say To That Is, Keep doing, Doing The Right Thing! Your Child Will Thank You Later and Love You Always.

If you are a donor, as I said before: "Don't Get Mad Get Even". Go one step above that real parent. Don't show your child(ren) that they are burdens/hindrances to you. Show them that you love them and that they can depend on you, as well. Think of it like this: There's a saying in the Bible that states: "When I was a child, I spake as a child; I thought as a child, I understood as a child but when I was older I put childish things away", to paraphrase. As a donor, your saying should be: "When I was a child I did childish things." "Now that I have a child, it's time to put childish and selfish things away. Why? Because guess what "My Child Comes First! Donors just don't care! Real parents do!

DONOR FAMILIES VS. REAL PARENT FAMILIES:

There is a great difference between "donor" families and "real" parent families.

Real parent families are just like the real parents. They become grand parents, nanas, pa-pas, aunts, uncles, cousins and extended families.

They help the real parent out with the things that they can't do at the time. They help with babysitting, they give the real parents support, love and even help them figure things out. They listen to the real parent vent, when they need to vent. They are the extra positive attention that the child needs. They become the child's heroes. In other words, they usually also become the second parents to the child. In some cases, it's the only side of a child's family that they get to really know. These are the people with whom the child becomes comfortable with in their lives. They also get to watch the child grow into the man or woman that they will become.

Donor families, aren't always around for the child(ren). The children may get to know a few but even then, they won't help. A friend once told me that: They guess that if you are not dealing with the donor, then the family doesn't want to have anything to do with the child(ren). I guess this means they are not obligated either. The child suffers, knowing only one side of the family and ends up, not knowing the donor families' history(medical, traditions, values, etc). Donor families need to get involved, before it's too late. The child(ren) did not do anything wrong by being born.

In some cases, the donor has messed up within its own family and they take it out on the child because of what the donor did to them, instead of getting to know the child as an individual.

My message to Donor families: please get to know the child! You don't want to wait until they are older or should the child(ren) become famous, then you want to come out the wood works calling them your relatives as often as this happens. Some donor families live right down the street from the child and won't do anything to help with the child. They won't speak or help the 15 real parent out in anyway.

The real parent tries to keep the lines of communication open, but eventually gets to the point of why? Why should I keep trying to force a relationship with these people when they do not care about the child. Real parents shouldn't have to ask the donor family to do anything. They should automatically, want to do it. The relationship they may have with the donor should not determine the relationship with the child(ren). If you have a good relationship with the donor, you should have a greater one with the child. If you have a bad relationship with the donor, or even possibly the real parent, d o not take it out on the child.

I have an associate who attends a church and she brings her child. At the church, the real parent, the real parents' family and some of the donors' family attend the same church, as well. The donor family was involved with the child, at first. But now, they offer no help, no phone calls, not even a hello. Now, if you cannot be hospitable in God's house or your Higher Powers' house, there is definitely something wrong with that picture!

Donor families, you need to be as positive, or have a greater influence or impact on that child's life. Get Involved, Positively!

WELFARE RECIPIENTS:

Welfare is one of the most touching subjects. It is such a sensitive matter in some cases, that impacts both the real parents as well as the donors. It is okay to use welfare, as it is needed, but it does not have to be a lifestyle. Use it as temporary help but not as a permanent way of life.

It is a tool to help get ahead or out of the economic situation that one might be in at the time. It's ideal to get a job or even a career or turn the job into a career. It does not matter if it's McDonald's or if eventually you become a doctor or a nurse. But, get off of welfare. Stop abusing the system!

There are real parents, as well as donors who think it's okay to just stay on welfare. It's Not! Child(ren) are watching and learning from the adults. A child is constantly needing and growing. And needing things more often than just sit once a month. There are some capable adults who just sit around, waiting on cash one day, and food stamps on another day. Then, there are some real parents that don't even spend the money or food stamps on the child. These real parents and donors have chosen a lifestyle of materialistic things such as: being the best dressed, or having the best car. The child ends up with nothing (i.e. no clothes, food, shoes, socks, medicine, etc). Ending up with nothing is not positive for the child. It is not teaching the child the value of hard work. Hard work has its own reward. "God Bless The Child That's Got Its Own."

There are some real parents and donors who have a value system and use the money for the things that the money is intended. As parents, or donors, children need to know that there is more to life than just a welfare system.

Donors more than likely are not teaching the child anything anyway.

So this does not apply to you. But real parents, true enough, welfare helps, but sometimes a chilld may think that it's okay to be on welfare, just sit around and have children and not work. Then, that's where that welfare recipient cycle may begin. It has to stop, somewhere. Why not with you?

My mom told her children, all the time: "Work, get a job, go to school, do something; and if you are not doing something positive, the system will give you something to do and some place to go(usually meaning jail)."

It is hard to see welfare given to real parents and donors who you know are abusing the system; especially, when there are real parents who get out and work daily, and still have needs yet, receive nothing from welfare. These parents are told that they make too much money.

They cannot even receive a little help. The counties base their decisions on that person's gross income, instead of what the working parent brings home, the needs of each child and the bills that the working parent has to pay.

Real working parents must budget their income, deciding what to pay or not to pay. The money has to be shuffled by priority; hopefully they can save for an emergency. But, sometimes that's even hard to do.

Parents and Donors just need to get up everyday, get out and do something. Don't teach our children that, it is okay to sit around, and just let the counties take care of them. Instill in them dedication, hardwork, values and morals.

Teach them responsibility and just maybe, when they have a child of their own, they will not be donors, but responsible, real parents.

NOT WANTING THE DONOR:

For some donors, it is hard for them to understand that, the real parent just does not want them. Most real parents just want the donor to be responsible for the child, and to not think because they ask for things strictly for the kids, that they want a relationship with them. What they want is for the parent to do for the child that they have together. Real parents don't want to be buttered-up, try to have sex with the donor or even want them touching them. The real parent does not want the donor trying to see who they are dating or even, know if they are dating or even if they are living with someone. The real parent doesn't want to hear the crap about:" I bet they can't /don't love you like I do /or did. The only conversation that should be between a real parent and donor is about the child.

Donors should stop questioning the child about what the real parent is doing, who they are dating or whatever. Guess What? It's None Of The Donors' Business! If the real parent wants the donor to know, they will let the donor know. The donor should only be involved in the dating scenario, if the person the real parent is dating is abusing your child. Yes, then that's when to get involved, but make sure you find out the facts, first. Donors, if the real parents don't want you, then let them go on with their lives, and just do for your child. Just accept the fact that you are not wanted. Tip: Just in case the real parent does have, lets say a "weak moment", and does sleep with you; the sex might just be out of pity. And who wants pity sex? Just in case the donor is a stalker, who can not believe that real parent has moved on in his/her life, there are restraining/protective orders. Do you really want to go to jail because you did not take care of your responsibility when you had the chance first; to be involved and do the right thing.

Don't jump up and fight the other parent. Especially not in front of the child. This definitely leads to dysfunction. The child thinks that it is okay to abuse your loved ones or to be abused by their loved ones. They begin to accept abuse and make that a part of their lives.

What happens if you end up killing the real parent'? Donor will end up in jail. What happens to the child? Whose going to be there to love them because you have killed the real parent? Whose going to be there to make sure the child has what he/she may need? Donor, you know your family will more than likely not help out with the child. You are in jail, you have killed the real parent. On the other side of that issue why would you want to put the real parent in the situation that they might possibly have to kill you because they had to protect themselves because you couldn't accept the fact that you are not wanted. Donors you know that you are not wanted but you stalk the real parent and the child to the point that they are living their lives in fear of you as a person. The real parent and child have to keep moving from place to place because they are afraid of you and what you might do to them. Why would you want your child to have an unstable life because of that fear?

As a donor, you have to realize when you are not wanted. Then move on with your life. There are plenty of other people that you can get involved with. Maybe, you won't make the same mistake that you made in the previous relationship. Get some help! Realize:" Donor Not Wanted!"

How To Become An Effective Parent If You Are A Donor:

GET INVOLVED! GET INVOLVED! GET INVOLVED! STEP UP AND BE RESPONSIBLE! TAKE RESPONSIBILTY! BE POSITIVE! STOP BEING

SELFISH!

Sorry about all the anger. But, no one should have to say these things to you. These are things that you should already know.

GET INVOLVED—Get involved in the things your child is doing or whatever things the child is involved with at the time. Show them that you are interested and that you love them daily. Call them to see how their day was. See if you can help with their homework or sometimes just listen to them. Have an open relationship with the real parent, so the child can feel safe with you. As a donor possibly taking the child for a few hours a week, overnight or maybe, eventually a vacation. But, there has to be trust between the real parent and the donor. Show your child that you are willing to do things for them and with them. Never look at your child as burdens or say you do not have time for them; or the things they are interested in. You never know what a child will remember when they get older. Wouldn't it be exciting for your child to remember you(donor) doing something positive and encouraging them.

BE RESPONSIBLE— You know the saying: You were responsible enough to lye there and get it; be responsible and take care of it." It's that plain and simple.

TAKE RESPONSIBILITY—Sperm Donors: "Man Up! Egg Donors: "Woman Up!" Get up and get a job if you don't have one. Even if its picking up cans, paper route or something. Spend your time and money on your child. Don't make the real parent do everything. Get a job where you can collect a check. Stop working "under the table" for cash. If you don't want all your money taken in child support then get two jobs: One that child support can take from and then the second one will give you more money for (watch this): You and your child. Earning money will assure you benefits and will also help you when you become older when your benefits for Social Security take effect. The benefits will help take care of your children if something happens to you (disability or death). If you "work under the table" all the time, you and your child lose out later. Just like a real parent has to try and save for the child's future, so, should you donor. There were two people there when the child was conceived. So, why can't there be two people to be responsible for the child. It applies even if you have more than one real parent. You know different kids with different parents. All your children should be receiving your money, love, support and encouragement. Take the child to church with you. Go to social events with your child {birthday parties, school functions, dinners, piano lessons, etc). I know that goes with getting involved.

BE POSITIVE—Always take the positive way with your child. Do positive things around them, with them, to them. Give them praise and encouragement when they do well and do positive things. Don't smoke, drink or curse around the child (or just not a lot). Those things should not be the only things they hear or see from you. Hug your children, laugh with them and especially at them when they are doing silly things. Make each moment with them special!

Never say anything bad about the real parent to the child or when they are in earshot. Be respectful because you do know you have to give respect in order to get respect. Don't have a bunch of people around your kids that are not doing positive things. Its okay to give up your friends for a while; when you are with your child/children. Real friends would understand that! Those friends that get upset, you might want to re-examine that friendship. Do I have to say it again? "Children First!"

STOP BEING SELFISH— It Is Not About You Anymore! It is about the kids. Make sure you are doing what your child needs you to do all the time. And that you are at least willing to give them what they need and want sometimes. Stop thinking about what you can get out of what you do for your child/children.

Don't worry about your child support money. PAY IT! If you don't want to give the extra money to the real parent. Go out and get what your child needs on your own. You at least know your kids need clothes, food, socks or pampers. Get those things just on principal. No one should have to force you to do at least these thh gs. You know what you need; what makes you think your child/ children don't need those items? I know repetition. I would not have to repeat it, if YOU JUST WAKE UP AND GET IT THROUGH YOUR HEAD! Stop flossing, like you are all that. When you know you are not doing what you should be doing for your kids. How dumb do you really feel at this point? Your kids are struggling and you are flossing.

How Not To Become A Donor?

Real parents keep doing the positive things you are doing to keep your child happy, motivated, and well taken care of with the things they need.

Don't let your donor or any other person bring you down. Don't let them steal your joy.

Don't allow negative things enter into you and your child/ children's life. For example (drugs, friends that mean you harm or any other negative things).

Because you never know the outcome of a situation and the consequences you think might happen, might be far worse. Then that means that your child would have to suffer.

I know there are days when you want to just throw in the towel or say "why does all my money go to bills or the kids?" "Why do I never get to have fun or a break?" "Why do I have to always be the responsible one?"

Well the question is answered when you look at your child/children face at the end of the night. When they are asleep without a care in the world and you know that the smile on their face is because of you and what God has blessed you with and given you the ability to do. The blessing is yours.

Just Because: (Miscellaneous)

Real parents do for the child what has to be done. Donors do what they want to do when they want to do for the child.

It is so wonderful to see your child wake up every morning. It's fun to play with them; or even watch them interact with other children as well. They will even show you as a real parent that they do pay attention to you. Your fussing, discipline, manners, educational matters or even how to help or care for others. Donors do not have this opportunity.

Why Should Your Child Have To Wait?

This is a question that haunts me to this day. When real parents hear the donor say that the child has to wait.

It is hard enough as real parent to even call or talk to the donor to ask or state that the child needs anything. As a real parent, you have already reached the boiling/desperation point that you even have to hear this. When as a real parent, you give your all from the beginning. It's just that you might be at a point where you have extinguished all your resources(money, food shelves, family support, etc). So you call the donor, as a last resort. And you get that response back. You get to hear the donor say, "oh, can you call me back on Thursday?" "I have some things to take care of and the child have to wait. It feels like a slap in the face. Then just to see what's gonna happen on Thursday or whatever day. You call and then you get the punch in the gut that the last resort is an idiot. And they only think of themselves. You know what should be done. The one thing that should have been done first. "Go To God." Rejoice Anyhow."

Donors, children should not have to always wait on your sorry asses. If the real parent calls you; don't act like they are bothering you. You say yes and do your damnest to get what needs to be done. The real parent does it everyday. If they ask you apparently they need it. The real parent usually knows that you are trifling and just need to sec if you would ever get involved or be responsible for your child, if they really need it. And as a donor, the answer usually is the child has to wait or just flat out no.

You should not make your child wait ever. You have to realize that you are saying "no" to your child. But, let your child say no to you for something and you will think they are being disrespectful.

Throughout the rest of this book, there are going to be scenarios that I hope will open everyone's eyes to reality. To teens, I hope that these scenarios will help you make great choices for yourself, your future, your child's future and happiness. Think about this if you had waited maybe the situation would be better for you and your child This applies to adults, too.

Real Parents: You Are Not Obligated To Your Donors:

As a real parent especially single ones, you are not obligated to your donor.

You are not responsible for the donor in any aspect. Especially, when they have not even helped you. So, don't fall for the guilt trips that they might try to lay on you. Ignore them like they ignore you. Think about the time when your child needed clothes, pampers, etc and you told the donor and the response was: no or can it wait, maybe another day! Think about the day when the child needed food and the donor was too trifling to even help. Think about when you had to skip a bill because your donor was too selfish to work or pay child support and your child had to do homework by candlelight while wrapped in as many blankets as possible because you had no help to pay the heating/light bill on time. Think about when you had to go without your medication because you had to take the child to the doctor and the child needed medicine and you couldn't get help with the co-payments because the donor has no obligations to help make medical/dental payments. So don't feel bad to tell them no when as an adult they go out in the world and mess up(get kicked out their place, need food, go to jail or whatever). Tell the donor the same no or maybe later that they tell you when you ask them for help. Sure, they will probably call you cold- hearted, evil, mean, and everything but a child of God. They might even say they wish you were dead or they wish God would strike you down. Just let it roll right off your back.

Their negative comments mean nothing to you, just like when the child needs, it means nothing to them. Be just as selfish as they are and just pray for them. Pray that they get their act together for themselves, Not on beliefs that you all are getting back together or anything. Pray that they learn to love and honor their child. Pray that you guys will be able to get along positively for the sake of the child. And even if they do say something that hurts you, don't let the donor push your buttons. "Don't Respond To Ignorance." "Don't get as ignorant as them." Always stay up and above them.

You already have the child; you don't need the extra stress of helping someone who never helps your child. Your cheeks ought to be pretty tired of being turned. "Let Go And Let God." As the saying goes: "You Are

Too Blessed To Be Stressed and Too Anointed To Be Disappointed". Halleujah, Amen!

Here comes the scenarios:

MAN UP!!

Maschelle and Donovan:

I Owe You Nothing

Maschelle, is a very bright, hardworking young lady. She's twenty-seven years old 5'7, Hispanic with long curly hair. She works two jobs and have no children. At her first job, she is a cashier at a convenience store. She has worked at this store for two years. She is pretty well known throughout the store and everyday different males ask her for her phone number and for dates She always laughs and states that she does not date and will not give out her number. At her second job, she works overnights in a department store doing overnight stock.

Maschelle is always working, she feels as if she does not have the time to date. So sometimes, when she's home alone, she will talk on the chatline whether, phone or internet. She feels that at least, that way she's flirting and sometimes "get off" when she needs to. She knows its hard to be lonely but she feels this is the safest way where she would have no children because she is not where she wants to be in her life and that she is just not ready.

One day, while talking and joking around with her other female co-workers a male customer that comes in everyday who frequently asks Maschelle out, came into the store. Like clockwork, he asks her out and for her phone number. Again, he is told 'no". So, he leaves sadly. Maschelle starts joking around with her co-workers again, and her friend Lisa asks her: "why does she always turn men down when they ask her out" '!The other ladies, chimed in, as well. Trying to figure out why she never told a man, "yes" or gave a man her number". Maschelle, stated: "she just wanted to wait on the right man to come along."

She told her co-workers how she was looking for a man that could accept the fact that she went to work, church and home. That's the lifestyle she lives right now. She knew that it would be hard in this day and age to find a man that would like a woman like her without trying to use or abuse her.

So, Maschelle's co-workers listened and they dared her to even talk to the next man that came in the door and to also give tlte man her phone number. Maschelle jokingly laughed, but accepted the dare. The next male customer, Named Donovan came through the door. Donovan was a 6'3, 215lbs, forty year old caucasian male. He smelled of Curve cologne and looked like he had been out all night. Maschelle's co-workers watched and snickered. Maschelle treated the man with the best customer service that she could, flirtatiously, and as she expected, he asked for her number and a date.

Maschelle smiled and gave him her cell phone number. He asked what time she would be getting off and she said 4:00 pro. Donovan, so sure about the date and excited, for himself, took his items and stated that he would call her at 4:30pm. Her co-workers clapped and cheered with excitement for Maschelle because they knew that it was hard for her to do that. Maschelle got off work at 4:00 pm and went shopping after work with her friend, Lisa. They were talking about the events of their day at work. They were in Macy's department store looking at Baby Phat outfits. Lisa stated: "girl, its 4:30 and your phone has not rung, I told you he was not gonna call you". The ladies chuckled, just then, around 4:33p.m. Maschelle's cell rings. Maschelle looks at the number. She did not recognize the number. Lisa jumps up and down screaming in the store. "It's Him, It's Him!" "I told you he was gonna call," Maschelle gives her a "whatever" look. She answers the phone and on the other end she hears Donovan's voice. He stated, "Hi beautiful, I told you I would call you. Maschelle smiled; and stated: "Yes you did". They talked while Lisa and Maschelle shopped. Donovan asks, "What are you doing right now?" Maschelle stated that she was shopping with her friend. Lisa is pulling on Maschelle's arm jumping up and down asking, "What is he saying?" "When are you guys going out? Maschelle whispers for Lisa to hush! Donovan and Maschelle continue to talk, until the ladies got to the register. Maschelle stated that she needed to get off the phone while the cashier rang her items. She stated that it would be rude to be on the phone when someone else was talking to her. Donovan said he understood and asked if it was okay if he called her later. Maschelle, stated, "yes'. The ladies purchased their items and went home.

Maschelle was exhausted from the day and since she had the night off, she decided she needed some "Shelle time". She turned her cell off, she made dinner and took a long hot steamy bath. She got on the chatline for a while ate and went to bed. Around 10:30 pm, she woke up and realized that her cell phone had not rung, all evening. So she went and checked it. She forgot that she had turned it off. She turned the phone on. She looked at the screen and realized she had 2 missed calls. They were from Donovan. Just as she was about to put the phone down, it rang. It was Donovan, again. "Hello Beautiful, How are you doing, asked Donovan. Maschelle stated that she was fine. And she apologized for missing his calls. "You are gonna live a long time," Maschelle stated. Why do you say that, Donovan asked. I was just turning my phone on and was about to put it down and you called. Well, what a coincidence, great minds think alike, Donovan said. Maschelle chuckled, I guess so. They talked on the phone for a few hours. Maschelle, stated how she had to get up early to go to work.

The next day as Maschelle was working; like clockwork Joel her everyday customer comes in, and again asks for her phone number. Again, she says "no". As she is talking to Joel a delivery person comes into the store with three dozen red roses. Everyone in the store was shocked as the man asked if there was a Maschelle who worked there. Lisa screamed, there she is and pointed down the candy aisle and said. "Schelle, girl these are for you'. "No girl, you have got to be kidding" Maschelle responded. As Maschelle opened the card, Joel sadly left. In all the excitement, she didn't realize he had gone. She read the card, it stated: 'Hello beautiful, I really had a great time last night. Maschelle smiled, no one had ever given her flowers before. Lisa said: he had a great time last night, Schelle did you give away your goodies last night"? Maschelle said," hell no" We, just talked on the phone. Sure, Lisa said, "tell me anything. You know, if you didn't give them up you know you want to. So, when are you guys going on a date"? Maschelle said that she didn't know. Maschelle got off from work, went home and put the roses in a vase and just stood back and admired their beauty. She took a nap, woke up around 8:00pm. She began preparing her dinner, showered and got ready for work.

She was so happy she just hummed all night, as she worked. She got off the next morning and had the day off at the convenience store. So, she got home and showered and exhaustily, put on her pj's and crawled into bed.

Just then her phone rang. Hey girl, it's me Lisa. I was just calling to check on you to make sure you got home safely. They lived on the same floor in the same apartment complex. They talked briefly and got off the phone. Maschelle went back to sleep. She slept until 2:00pm. She woke up and started making dinner. She made enough for herself and Lisa and Lisa's family. Lisa, a single mother. She is Caucasian and has twin daughters: Aisha and Ashley. So, Maschelle would cook for them when she was off from the day job. She always made enough so Lisa wouldn't have to cook and she could focus on her daughters. Just as she finished, her cell rang. It was Donovan. They talked for a while and laughed and just as Maschelle was in mid laughter from something he said, Donovan asked Maschelle out on a date. They had been talking on the phone everyday.

Maschelle, stated that she would go. She stated that she was off from her night job on Saturday and that it would be great to go out with Donovan.

Saturday

Maschelle woke up early on Saturday. She wanted to get a new outfit for her date with Donovan. She asked him what she should wear. He told her to dress nicely. So she went and bought a Baby Phat dress. Maschelle loved Baby Phat clothes. She got home and took a nap so she could be rested for her dinner date.

Donovan arrived at 8:00pm. He knocked on the door with three dozen yellow Roses with one single red rose in the middle. Maschelle opened the door and just burst into tears. She was so overwhelmed. It was her first date, in a long time. She took the flowers in the house and her friend Lisa who helped her get dressed, screamed in excitement and took the flowers and put them in a vase for Maschelle.

Maschelle walked back out. Lisa screamed, "Girl, don't you do anything I would do." They both just laughed. Donovan escorted Maschelle to the car. They drove to Donovan's and they talked, laughed and listened to music, all the way there. When they arrived Maschelle noticed that there were rose petals all the way to the door. Donovan joked, "Excuse the mess."

They both laughed. Once the door was opened, Maschelle was shocked with the date of her dreams. She finished walking in and began to cry. Donovan asked: "What's wrong Maschelle, why are you crying?" She just replied," it's beautiful." In the middle of the floor was the most beautiful picnic, ever. There were roses all over the room. There was champagne and flutes, a chocolate fountain with milk chocolate flowing. There was fresh fruit, cheese and crackers and Maschelle's name written with rose petals. Donovan helped her onto the floor and told her to get comfortable and that he would be right back. He went into the kitchen and came back with two plates of shrimp and chicken alfredo with creamy alfredo sauce with spinach. Maschelle asked, "you made this?" And Donovan answered, "yes". Maschelle was very impressed. She couldn't believe that he had done all of this. She explained to Donovan, the reason that she cried, when she first walked into the house. She explained that she always dreamed of this picnic, as a first date. She stated that she would pray that she would find the man of her dreams who would on their first date would have a romantic picnic. That man would know her, inside and out. And she wouldn't have to say anything. He would just know.

They laughed and talked about everything. Maschelle told him that her birthday was in three weeks. They ended up just curled up on the couch and fell asleep. Maschelle woke up around 2:00 am and woke Donovan up to take her home. So he did he drove her home and explained to her on the way there, that the flowers meant something, too. They meant that no matter what happened they would be friends and the one single red rose represented the love they would hopefully, one day share. He gave her a goodnight kiss and watched as she went into the apartment. She flicked the light on and off to let him know that she was in safely.

The next few weeks were wonderful! They saw each other all the time; and talked everyday.

On Maschelle's birthday, they went to Jamaica. He surprised her with the tickets, the week prior and her bosses gave her the time off since she was such a good employee and never took time off.

Jamaica was truly beautiful! They saw a lot of sights, had a driver chauffeur them to numerous places. They even went to Dunn's River Falls. They had a cottage (chalet), right on the beach. They spent seven glorious days there.

Their last night there, which was actually Maschelle's birthday; they made love. There was so much passion that they exhaustily, fell asleep.

They arrived home and Lisa picked Maschelle up from the airport. They talked on the way home. Maschelle told her everything about the trip. Lisa said, "girl good, if anyone deserves some good dick, its you. It's time you got rid of those cobwebs." They both laughed.

Maschelle and Donovan decided to date, exclusively. They took walks in the park, fed the ducks, spent nights at each other's homes. They spent all their free time together. Before they knew it, months had passed by. Maschelle had started feeling sick and noticed that "aunt flow" had not made her monthly visit. She let another week go by and then she began to panic. She talked to Lisa and expressed her concerns. So Lisa came over with a pregnancy test. Maschelle went to take the test, it was positive.

Maschelle and Lisa both screamed. Lisa asked Maschelle what was she gonna do. Maschelle could not do anything but cry. She made Lisa promise not to tell anyone until she verified it from a doctor, especially not tell Donovan. She didn't know how she was gonna tell him. The next day Maschelle called and made a doctor's appointment for the following day.

Next Day

Maschelle and Lisa went to the appointment and the doctor confirmed that Maschelle was pregnant. Maschelle thanked the doctor and made her next appointment. Maschelle went home, took a hot bubble bath and took a nap before she went to work. She got up later and made lunch for herself and went to work, but, she could not get the thought out of her head, that she was pregnant. She left work the next morning and ran home quickly to prepare for her day job. When she got there Lisa smiled and asked how she was doing. Maschelle stated, she was fine; that she was just tired because she had just gotten off her night job and came straight to work. They went on a break a few hours later. Lisa asked; "Schelle did you tell Donovan yet?" Maschelle said "no", she did not know how to tell him. As they went back to work, Joel came and started his daily conversation with Maschelle. He asked if she was feeling ok. Maschelle threw up right at that moment. She rushed to the bathroom with Lisa and Joel in tow. Maschelle just cried, and cried. Joel and Lisa knocked on the door." Schelle, Schelle, are you ok", they asked. I'm fine, Maschelle said cryingly as she tried to sound ok. She washed her face and came out with a huge smile on her face. Joel asked: "are you ok?" He saw that she was smiling and said: "There's that beautiful smile that brightens my day." Just then the manager came over to check out the situation. "Is everything okay over here?" Maschelle and Lisa stated yes and got ready to go back to work. Joel left and stated that he might come back later to check on Maschelle. Maschellc asked her manager if she could talk to her privately. Maschelle explained to her manager that she was pregnant and also that she had not told the father yet. The manager understood and Maschelle got up and went back to work. Later that day, Joel came back to the store. He talked to Maschelle for a while. She asked him a hypothetical question. If you were dating a female and she found out she was pregnant when would you want her to tell you? Joel answered: immediately!

He asked, 'is that what's going on with you?" Holding back tears Maschelle said: "yes". She apologized to Joel because she knew that he was there everyday waiting for her to say "yes" to a date with him. Joel just hugged her and said; "no need to apologize." You have a blessing growing in you and you don't need to cry or stress yourself out. Fighting back tears himself, Joel told her to go back to work and told her she would be fine. Joel left and went back to work. He immediately started praying for Maschelle when he got back to his office across the street. *"Father I come to you as humbly as I know how. Icome praying for Maschelle. I pray for strength for myself, as well as her. I pray that she has a great pregnancy. And t hat I will be man enough for when your will is done and the plan unfolds, we will be able to both grow in you. Prepare her Lord to be strong, virtuous and humble. Build her up where she's weak, Lord. Keep walking with her daily and when the situation gets rough, Lord, I know you will carry her through. My prayer Lord is for her to be my wife, pregnant or not. I Love Her Lord, as I Love You and the church. Lord let your will be done. These and other blessings I ask in your son, Jesus' name. Amen.* After he got done praying, he worked until 6p.m. and left. Joel is a six foot four two hundred and fifteen lbs, African American male with pretty pearly white teeth. He is well educated and just as seas they come. Maschelle got off from work and went home to nap before work. She was so exhausted from the day. About 8:oopm her cell rings. "Hey beautiful, I'm sorry that you have not heard from me in a few days. I had to go to Dallas. I missed you so much, what's new?" Maschelle began to cry and Donovan asked what was wrong? Maschelle asked if he could come by the next day she had to talk to him about something important. He said: "sure". Maschelle went to her night job and when she made it home to change, Donovan was sitting in his truck outside. Maschelle knocked on the window of the truck and asked: "Why are you here this early?" Donovan said: "you sounded worried on the phone and I couldn't sleep so I just thought I would meet you before you went to work. Come and sit

and talk to me." Maschelle stated that she needed to change clothes and invited Donovan up to her apartment. Lisa and her daughters were coming out as they passed her door. Lisa spoke to them and in unisom, the girls spoke "Hi, Aunt Maschelle, hello Mr. Donovan." Lisa pulled Maschelle to the side and asked if she had told him about the pregnancy. Maschelle stated that she was on her way to do just that, and that she would talk to her when she got to work.

. . . . I'm Pregnant . . . .

Maschelle and Donovan entered the apartment. Maschelle asked Donovan if he needed something to drink or anything. Donovan said: "no thanks." So, Schelle what do you have to tell me that is so important? Maschelle sat down by Donovan and took him by his hand and put it on her stomach. Donovan confusingly asked: "What's going on Maschelle?"' Maschelle told him she was pregnant with his child and that she must have gotten pregnant on her birthday. She told him all about "aunt flow" missing in action, about her being sick everyday, the home pregnancy test as well as the doctor's appointment. She told him that she planned to keep the baby because she didn't believe in abortion and she knew that God was giving her a blessing. To Maschelle's surprise, Donovan was speechless. He snatched away from Maschelle and took off out the door. Maschelle went after him but by the time she made it to the front door, Donovan's truck was pulling off. Maschelle didn't know what to do. She took a quick shower, cried and went to work.

When she got to work Lisa was waiting anxiously to talk to her. "Schelle, how did it go? Did you tell him? Schelle, Schelle, say something." Schelle couldn't say anything. She felt so numb. Lisa, Maschelle stated: "yes, I told him, and all he did was run out of my apartment." Lisa said: "I am so sorry Schelle." "Did you call him," Lisa asked. "No, I did not call him," Maschelle said:" I thought he would be happy, but apparently he's not. I have this blessing growing inside of me; and I am gonna "woman up" and do what I have to do." "If he's there, he's there." "If he's not then he's not." A few hours later Joel came in for his lunch break. He saw Maschelle and asked if she was feeling better today and if she had talked to Donovan. She answered "yes" to both questions."

Joel asked:" what was his response and Maschelle stated that: he just left, and no I did not call him." Joel asked:" How did you know that was my next question?""It seems to be everyone's next question said Maschelle. They both laughed. He gave her a hug and went back to work. Maschelle felt much better after talking with Joel. She went back to work with a smile on her face. She went home and took a nap to prepare to go to work that night. Maschelle went to work that night.

The next morning, Maschelle was off from her morning job. When she got home there was a message on her home phone. It was from Donovan. She was shocked and mad at the same time. She wondered why didn't he just call her cell? He never called her home phone. The message stated that he loved her and that he was not the father of her baby and to never contact him again. This pissed Maschelle off because she had opened up her heart to this man and during the first rough patch that they hit, he left. She cried herself to sleep. She got up around 3:00p.m. and started cooking. She made enough for Lisa, Aisha, and Ashley which was routine for them. Lisa and the girls arrived around 5:00p.m. Maschelle had made a wonderful dinner. The girls played cards, as Lisa and Maschelle talked. Maschelle told Lisa about the message. Lisa got mad: "No he did not go there." Girl, don't worry I am here for you and your baby everything will be fine. Be Strong! God's got you! Maschelle was comforted. "Hey Schelle", Lisa said:Joel came by today. Of course, he asked about his girl and her beautiful smile. I said: "Here I Am" and we both laughed. He told me to give you this and she reached in her purse and pulled out a card. It had his name and phone information on it. The card read Joel Anderson(attorney at law). On the back of the card he had wrote Proverbs 31 and stated for her to read it everyday. She smiled because it was one of her favorite scriptures to read in the Bible. Maschelle smiled and said: "Thank You Lord." Lisa asked what was that all about. Maschelle stated that he gave her a comforting word. Lisa said okay girl, we are gonna go because I know you have to go to work, see you tomorrow."

Months passed. Maschelle invested in maternity books and parenting books. She lived her life getting bigger and stronger everyday. Joel and Lisa were with her everyday. Joel kept praying for her. One night, Maschelle had worked her night job. When she got home Lisa, was at her door. Girl, we need to talk.

Where are the girls? Maschelle asked? Oh, they are watching television in the apartment. I will be quick. I saw Donovan yesterday when you were not at work. He had the balls to walk in and not speak. Girl, you know I snapped.

I asked him, "why you gonna make Schelle do this alone? She loved you. He couldn't say nothing. I called him a "sperm donor". I just cried. He talking about he was hurting everyday for what he was doing to you. He sounded so sincere so, I told him to call and talk to you, please don't be mad. She said Lisa it's fine, I'm not mad. But I'm not putting my life on hold waiting for him to get it together. am 5 months pregnant now, and am going today to find out what I am having, do you want to go? No one is gonna "steal my joy" today. Lisa stated: "I will be honored to go. Just let me get the girls dressed and off to school."

Maschelle and Lisa went to see Dr. Fall and she told Maschelle she was having a little girl. Maschelle and Lisa screamed and cried with excitement. They left and went to get ice cream. At the ice cream shop, they bumped into Donovan. Shockingly, he spoke to Lisa and tried to stop Maschelle and talk to her. "Maschelle, please stop and talk to me." Maschelle kept walking, as if she never heard him. He followed them into the ice cream shop. Lisa following behind them, Donovan entered the shop. "Maschelle, please, please talk to me," he said.

Maschelle stood there holding back tears and ordered her a chocolate chip cookie dough waffle cone. She sat at a table and Lisa joined her, asking "Schelle, are you gonna talk to him." Maschelle never answered. "You look beautiful Maschelle," Donovan said. She continued to eat her ice cream. Donovan kept talking like he was all concerned. "How are you Schelle?"

"Are things okay? "Have you found out the sex of the baby yet?" Lisa couldn't believe Masehelle was so calm.

"Are you gonna answer him at all Schelle?", Lisa asked. Maschelle asked Lisa Are you done with your ice cream?" Lisa said "yes." Maschelle said well let's go. Donovan watched them walk away and get into the car. "Why didn't you say anything" Lisa asked? Maschelle said: "I told you no one was gonna steal my joy today. I am thrilled to be having a daughter. Remember, it's not his child, anyway." "Girl, you are better than me, I would have gone off in there."

They would have had to put me out the place." Maschelle laughed: "Girl, you are so silly." They made it home and Lisa cooked at her apartment; so Maschelle ate over there. When Maschelle got home, there were three messages. One was from Joel he was checking on her and she had told him she was gonna find out the sex of the baby today. The other two were of course from Donovan: "It was good to see you Schelle." I have never stopped loving you. "Please give me a call." The second one he asked if she would join him for dinner, so they could talk. Maschelle laughed and thought Wow! He didn't want me to contact him but because he saw me, he wants to be around me and contact me. Wow! How ironic is that? Maschelle went to bed; she didn't have to work that night. She went to sleep thinking about names for her daughter.

2 months later . . . .

After numerous calls from Dononvan and Maschelle, ignoring them, she finally gave in and answered the phone. She listened to what he had to say. He was talking about how he was gonna help with the baby. He kept talking about how he loved her and wanted the best for her and the baby. He just wanted a chance. She gave him two weeks to see what he would do. In those two weeks, he did nothing. He had lied again. Maschelle just gave up on him. Life in other words was going great for Maschelle. She went to work, church and home. She kept her appointments. Schelle, Joel, and Lisa had planned to go to dinner together. Lisa had found a sitter, Maschelle's mom Ann. Joel had stated beforehand that he was paying for their nightout. Just as Maschelle was about to walk out her door. An envelope was slid under her door. Oh, Lord what now, Maschelle asked: But, when she opened the envelope she was shocked, in the envelope, there was a note and some pictures. It was a letter from Donovan's ex—wife and she had sent pictures of her kids. The letter stated who she was and that she lived in Dallas and that she was divorcing Donovan because he was a cheat, and that she was trying to warn Maschelle that he was a "sperm donor". She further stated that, he was selfish and that he didn't do anything for their kids; even when he came to Dallas, he never even came to see them. She wrote how he wouldn't work, so he didn't have to pay child support. She wrote Maschelle that she had hired a private investigator and that she knew that Maschelle was pregnant. She warned Maschelle not to let Donovan do these things to her. Maschelle was completely taken away. She looked at the pictures of the kids and just began to scream. She was trying to be strong throughout this pregnancy and tonight of all nights, this had to happen. The ex-wife put her phone number on the letter and asked Maschelle to call her. Maschelle folded the letter and put it in her purse. She was just about to open the door when she heard a knock. It was Lisa. "Girl, you ready? If not, I sure am. I am about to get my grub on. I starved myself today, for this. Girl, did he say where we were going? Schelle, girl do you hear me?" Maschelle jumped and said: "oh yeah, I hear you Lisa! You know you're crazy. Girl, lets go. The ladies stepped out of the apartment building door. They were so busy talking that they didn't even see the limo and driver holding a sign with their names on it. They looked up at the same time and their jaws just dropped. Lisa ran to the limo driver and sa id "for me" oh, "you shouldn't have". The driver laughed and opened the door. Once inside the limo there was a single yellow rose that had Lisa's name on it. And there were five dozen long stem red roses with Maschelle's name on it. They both just laughed. Lisa exclaimed, Girl, you see this limo, fully stocked? I'm about to get my drink on! Man, Joel sure is going out for someone who just gives him a beautiful smile." Maschelle said. "whatever, Lisa." They arrived at the restaurant, It was beautiful from the table cloths to the candles. It felt so warm in the restaurant. Once inside, the hostess asked their names and showed them to the table where Joel was standing waiting for them and said:" Good to see you all made it safely.." "We sure did," said Lisa. Thank you! Yes, thank you so much for everything. The limo, flowers and everything. It was wonderful. Joel said: "you arc welcome. Only the best for you Maschelle, you deserve it!" Just then Lisa said:" oh no, its not." Maschelle and Joel looked at her. What's wrong'? Turn around, it's Donovan.

Maschelle was enraged, Wow! "Not today, "she said. "You know what, excuse me. I've been quiet too long. She got up and went to where they were seated. Lisa and Joel went after her. "Schelle, no don't do it." Just then Donovan looked up. "Hello Donovan, hello Donovan's date. "How are things?" she asked, calmly. What's up Maschelle? This is Iesha. Maschelle laughed and said: "its so funny. I'm not even here to talk to you. l came to warn your date to run as fast as she can. To tell her how it is not even worth getting involved with you. So please, please listen. Let me tell you about Mr. Donovan here. My name is Maschelle and I am having Donovan's, daughter. He wined and dined me, took me to Jamaica, and everything and once I told him I was pregnant, he left. I did not hear from him, for months." Iesha got up Maschelle pleaded with her. "Please sit and listen so that way you will have the whole story. See, I saw him the day I found out that I was having a girl and I never responded to him. He called me everyday after that. I finally took a call two weeks ago and he was promising me how he was gonna help me with the baby. Mainly lying, I haven't seen anything or heard from him. Then guess what, Maschelle, said laughing. "On my way here, there was this package slid under my door." Schelle slammed the letter and pictures down. Donovan screamed, 'what's this?" Maschelle grinned, and said:" it's a letter from you r ex—wife. It's pictures of your kids. You know the ones you did not see when you were in Dallas. When you got back that's when I told you I was pregnant. Wow! Trifiling, huh? Not only does she state how you won't work legally that you are a "sperm donor" and don't even take ca re of your responsibilities. Oh, and she wanted to let me know that you have a private investigator following you. So how's that? Like I said, I wanted to warn you. Ms. Iesha, nice to meet you. Enjoy your dinner. I would order the lobster, if I were you. Now, if you both would excuse me. l have to go to my dinner guests." They all walked back to their table. Lisa said:" Maschelle wow, I am so proud of you. I'm glad you had the opportunity to get that out." "I know it was difficult," said Joel. And you did it with class!

A few minutes later, Iesha threw her glass of champagne in Donovan's face.! "Sperm Donor". She walked over to Maschelle and said, "thanks girl".

Joel, Lisa and Maschelle finished their dinner. When they finished they ordered dessert. Just then a marachi band came into the door and talked to the hostess and began playing, 'When God Gave Me You." and came over to their table. Lisa and Maschelle were amazed. Just then, their dessert came. Maschelle looked at her dessert and saw the red roses on the plate that said, "Will you?" And she looked up and Lisa was screaming, by this time as she looked at Joel who was on one knee with a 5karat Princess cut diamond ring in a platinum setting, and Joel said "marry me". Maschelle held her stomach and looked confused. Maschelle asked, Joel, what's going on? Why do? Are you sure, me? She couldn't get a sentence out. Joel got off his Knee. He said: let me tell you, why you."

Everyday after thanking God for the day and after my daily devotion.

Maschelle, you are all I think about. I pray for you hourly, daily. When I see my wife in my dreams; I see your face, your smile. When we hug, I feel your heartbeat. I miss you when I'm not around you. I think of you constantly.

I cannot imagine my life without you. I've grown more and more in love with you everyday. I've watched you grow so much spiritually, mentally and emotionally. And if you would allow me the opportunity, I would be honoured to be your husband and a father to your baby, and one day start a family of our own. I want us to grow old together; and watch our love grow everyday! But, if you want to think about it, please take the ring anyway. Schelle I love you and I do not want to put any more pressure on you. Just don't say "no". I know you've had a rough night. So let's finish dessert and get you ladies home." Lisa cryingly said: "Schelle, girl this man has poured his heart and soul out to you. And do you see the ring, 5 karats. Do you know what a woman has to do to get a 5 karat ring? All you have given him is a smile daily and some conversation. If you do not say yes, I will." They all laughed! Maschelle responded to Joel and said "I am truly honored that you see me as your wife; and the ring is extremely beautiful! You have been a part of my life, when no one else was there. You have shown me kindness, respect, love understanding and patience. I read Proverbs 31 daily, thanks to you. I have learned to be a virtuous woman. So, it will be my pleasure and I am honored to say: yes, I will marry you and become your life. But, can I get the baby out first? I cannot get married with swollen feet." They all laughed. Joel with tears in his eyes said: "thanks, you have made me the happiest man alive. You can have whatever your heart desires." He put the ring on her finger and kissed her, gently. The ladies prepared to leave. So, Joel walked them outside to the limo. The ladies thanked him and as the limo pulled off, Maschelle said: "Stop the car!" She jumped out of the car, ran to Joel and said: "thanks for being a hopeless romantic you are my knight in shining armor! I cannot wait to be your wife." She got back in the car and the ladies went home.

The next morning, Maschelle woke up. She went to visit her mom. Her mother opened the door and gave her daughter a hug saying: "Schelle, you are over kind of early is everything okay Mom, everything is wonderful and she put her hand on her cheek. Her mom didn't notice the ring. "Would you like some tea dear?" Yes, "mom." Her mom put on the kettle and looked in the cabinet for the tea bags. How's my granddaughter? Oh, mom she is healthy and we are doing great. Maschelle rubbed her stomach. The sunlight hit the ring just right and her mom screamed and jumped up and down. "You're engaged! Schelle, Schelle you are gonna make a beautiful bride. We gotta find a planner, get flowers, and caterers. Mom slow down, Schelle said. Can I get this baby delivered and settled first? Oh, Schelle, I'm sorry I guess I Just got caught up in the moment. So, whose the lucky man? I know its not Donovan, he has "sperm donor" written all over him. "No, mom you are right; it's not Donovan. And you are correct he is a "sperm donor". And she showed her mom the letter and the pictures that she had received the night before and told her everything that happened, even the proposal. Mom asked, So what are you gonna do?" I'm gonna call her to let her know I received the information and to let her know that I want us to stay in touch since the kids are brothers and sisters. They need to know each other and maybe let her know that Donovan and I could never be together again." "Wow, Schelle I have to say I am impressed with

the woman you have become, Ann said. You are handling the situation quite well. Anyway, tell me about the proposal again, that was simply the most romantic thing that I have heard." I know, Maschelle said. If I weren't pregnant, I probably would have fallen out of my chair. They both laughed and drank their tea. They spent the rest of the visit looking at baby pictures of Maschelle. "I think I turned out, great, mom. You did an outstanding job and I love you so much! Thank you." "You are welcome dear. I sure did, her mom said. Well, mom its been fun but I need to get home so I can go to work tonight. Now, that I am so far in my pregnancy they just have me sitting and scanning the items onto the floor.

Maschelle went to work that night, happy as ever. The next morning, Maschelle got off from work and went home to change for her day job.

She noticed her message light on the phone was blinking. She regretted checking it; it was Donovan. The message said: "Schelle, the way you behaved the other night was ridiculous. But, I must say no one has ever tried to put me in my place, like that before. But you can go ahead and raise your bastard child on your own. And you can tell my ex—wife the same thing. I do not have time for kids or the money to give to any kids, either." Usually, Maschelle would have responded. But, she just got ready and went to work. She couldn't wait to see Joel. She walked into work and everyone was smiling. Lisa, I swear you can't keep a secret to save your life. Lisa responded but it was so beautiful! Just then Joel walked in and everyone yelled, Congratulations! "Sir, you are getting a wonderful woman. He responded: "no, I am getting the best wife." They all agreed in unison. He talked to Maschelle for a while then kissed her and went back to work.

. . . . A few weeks later . . . .

Maschelle and Joel were getting to know each other more and more. He treated her like a queen and she tried not to let the dumb messages that Donovan had started leaving bother her or destroy the blessings she had in her life. Joel, Lisa and her mom came by everyday that Maschelle did not work to check on her, To make sure that she was okay because she was getting so close to her due date.

. . . . HAPPY BIRTHDAY . . . .

On August 1, Maschelle was sitting at home with Joel. They were ordering things online for the baby. When there was a knock on the door. She thought it was Lisa so she said "come on in Lisa." Just then the door opened and Donovan walked in the door. We're in here on the computer; Lis come on in. She looked up and to her surprise, she said, "What are you doing here?" she asked, "Didn't you hear my messages." "1ignore them for a reason," Maschelle said and told Donovan to get out. "I'm here with my fiance." She was pushing Donovan out the door. Just then she screamed," Oh God no!" Joel jumped up and said, "What's wrong Schelle?" "I think my water just broke". Just then Lisa was coming down the hall and asked; "What's going on? Donovan, why are you here?" Lisa, I think my water just broke." "Get out the way Donovan." Joel, lets get her to the ca r. "Lisa her bag is in the closet Joel said." I'm going too, Donovan said. "No, I don't want you there! Go away!" Lisa called Maschelle's mom to tell her to meet Maschelle and Joel at the hospital. "I deserve to be a part of this," Donovan said. This is my child, they all just walked past him and got into the car. They sped off in route to the hospital. They burst through the doors at the hospital. Donovan had followed in his truck. Schelle, I'm the father", Donovan said. Just then Maschelle's mom, Ann walked in. "What's going on? Donovan, why are you h ere?", she asked. Joel explained how Donovan had just popped over and that Maschelle was pushing him out the door and went into labor. Ew, boy i'm gonna Ann said. Mom,

Schelle said. I'm sorry baby how are you, Ann asked Maschelle? "I'm scared", Maschelle told her mother. The nurse took Maschelle to the room and got her comfortable and set up on the monitors. Outside the room, Joel finally said something to Donovan." Look man, that is my fiancé in there and right now she needs me.

You had the chance from day one to step up and be the father that you are suppose to be. You've lied, made empty promises, denied the baby and just all out disrespected my queen(my blessing) and the blessing that God blessed you with. Now, you want to come around. Well, no more! This will be your last day of hurting Schelle. And you know the saying; "you don't miss your water until the well runs dry." And the other one; "one man'sjunk is another man's treasure,". You have torn this woman down and God and I lifted her back up. So, you don't deserve to be here and now is not the time to try and be daddy. You are welcome to stay but this is me and Maschelle from now on. You will never hurt or disrespect her or your baby, again. Now, have a seat and let Maschelle run things. She's been in control all this time while you were out being a little boy. You are pathetic, your opportunity is missed and I am gonna make sure you pay support for that little girl! Joel walked into the delivery room where Maschelle and her mom were and was told, "its almost time." Lisa, Aisha and Ashley had made it by then. They were in the waiting room with

Donovan. Donovan tried to explain things to Lisa, she slapped him. You see the problem mth you is you are not happy so, you don't want to see others happy. Get over yourself We're having a baby!

They were there, for hours. Just then Joel came out. She's dilated to 10 cm.

And she is holding her own. "Can I see her," Donovan asked? No! Lisa and Joel said in unison. Her mom is the only person she wants in there. In the delivery room, Dr. Fall and the nurses got ready to deliver the baby.

The nurses and her mom helped Maschelle with her breathing and told her when to push. "Push!" said Dr. Fall, "Maschelle you are doing great! One more push!" Maschelle, pushed very hard and then she heard crying. Congratulations! Maschelle, you have a beautiful baby girl. It's 8:15pm. The nurse held the baby up so Maschelle and her mother could see her. They were both crying.

The nurse took the baby to clean, warm and weigh her. She's 8 lbs 2 oz. and very healthy. "You did it Schelle!" Her mom said: she's beautiful, "What are you gonna name her?" I will tell you when Joel and Lisa get in here.

Twenty minutes later, Joel and Lisa came into the room. "Wow, Schelle she is beautiful and so are you. Are you ok?" asked Joel. "Yes, I have my family here with me," said Maschelle. Ann said," well they are in here now. What are you naming your daughter?" Maschelle responded: I have decided to name her Jalicia after the two of you Joel and Lisa. Her middle name is gonna be Ann after you momma. Just then there was a knock on the door.

Everyone sighed, it was Donovan. Can I see her? Maschelle did not feel like arguing, so she said "okay." But, they watched him like a hawk. He said thanks, kissed Jalicia and left.

Maschelle stayed in the hospital for two days and then was discharged. Joel came to pick her up. He took her and the baby to his house. Maschelle said: "Joel, I want to go home, I'm tired." He said:" you are home." He helped her out the truck and helped get Jalicia and her things out of the truck. "What's going on Joel?" Maschelle asked. This is your new home.

Joel "this is too much!" Nothing is too much for my queen and our new little princess. Maschelle walked in and there was her mom, Lisa, Aisha and Ashley. You guys! 'What are you all doing here? They helped me move your stuff here and helped me set up the nursery for Jalicia. Maschelle cried." Don't worry about anything," said Lisa "enjoy being happy!" I called both of your jobs for you. And everything is fine. We are gonna miss you in the apartment building. Just then, Joel said, "what do you mean?" Well, I know how much you mean to Maschelle and I've paid a years rent for you and your daughters to move across the street. And mom, you have a room here and are welcome over anytime. And feel free to stay and help Maschelle get adjusted to the baby and being here. Maschelle said, "I don't want to live in sin." Joel stated, "you won't. You have a room right off the nursery until we get married. See, sex is not important to me. When we get married I want the experience of making love to my wife. I could have had sex anytime with anybody. I dedicated myself to you." Maschelle could not say anything. She was so overwhelmed and exhausted that she just wanted to take a nap. As she and the baby slept, Joel made dinner for them.

2 weeks later . . . .

Lisa and the girls moved across the street. She had been thanking Joel everyday for what he did. She forwarded her mail and filled out your forwarded mail application for Maschelle. After work, Lisa came over to visit Maschelle and Jalicia. "All moved in," Maschelle asked Lisa. "Yeah, girl finally." How are you and Jalicia doing?" We are adjusting. Girl, this feels like a dream. I can't believe this is happening. "When are we gonna start planning our wedding? Our wedding? Lisa just laughed. Soon,

Maschelle said: "Well, I need to get dinner started. Joel has been spoiling me and Jalicia so much. I think its time to return the favor." "Yeah, girls carats you're suppose to cook everyday," Lisa said: They both just laughed. Lisa got ready to leave. Bye, Schelle, Bye Jalicia. I'll see you guys later. Let me get to these girls. Maschelle prepared dinner for Joel and herself. She prepared the table and put Jalicia in her portable bassinet right beside the dinner table. Just as she was setting the last plate. Joel walked in smiling.

He said: "it smells wonderful in here. And look at my girls. Hi Jalicia how are you doing today?" He kissed Maschelle. I didn't think you could cook.

You worked two jobs and everything, I figured that you ordered out. Maschelle smiled. I see someone has jokes. They ate dinner and talked about the events of the day. Just then Joel said:" oh Maschelle I forgot to give you your mail from the old place. Maschelle said:" thanks." She looked through the envelopes and one was from the county courthouse. Maschelle didn't understand why she was getting a letter from the court. So, she opened the letter and began reading it. The letter fell to the floor and Maschelle just began bawling. What's wrong? Joel picked the letter up off the floor and began skimming through it. The letter stated that Donovan wanted joint custody of Jalicia and his visitation rights put into play. Why won't he just leave us alone? I gave him every opportunity to be a father and to be in Jalicia's life. He's the one that ran away from his responsibilities. Joel seeing his fiance was so upset, told her to just go upstairs and calm down. Go take a relaxing bath and lay down. I'll take care of Jalicia and the dishes. Don't give him the victory of being upset.

Remember, I am an attorney and I sit on a board of lawyers. I know the best family court attorney in the state. I will pull some strings and see what I can come up with.

A week later, Joel came home with an attorney. Maschelle this is Ms. Coleman. Ms. Coleman, this is my fiance Maschelle. How are you doing, Maschelle? Joel has told me about the case and I am willing to do it for you all pro bono.

Maschelle and Ms. Coleman talked for the next couple of weeks. "I feel that we have a very strong case." Ms. Coleman stated. Although, he will probably try to use the fact that you are engaged to dispute the financial side of it.

But, It shouldn't hold up in court. Because Jalicia is his responsibility. And plus I have a trick or two up my sleeve.

.... A Month Later ....

.... Court Day ....

It's Monday, 10:00 am. Maschelle and Ms. Coleman walk into the family court building. They go through security and are told what floor and room number their case will be heard and that their case will be heard in front of Judge Cone. Ms. Coleman stated how Judge Cone was but that she was well respected in the court system and how fair she was. Maschelle was nervous. But, Ms. Coleman assured her not to worry and that they had a strong case. Don't worry! You have your receipts. We have witnesses on your behalf, you have me and you have your surprise witness. Maschelle looked at Ms. Coleman, "surprise witness? what surprise witness?" Don't worry.

Here, call your mother and check on Jalicia. Maschelle's mom was watching Jalicia while they were at court. While Maschelle was on the phone she saw Lisa and Joel come in. They were her witnesses for everything. Ms. Coleman had a video statement from Maschelle's mother. Donovan came in. He was with his attorney.

Donovan introduced his attorney, Mr. Hardiman to Ms. Coleman and Maschelle. The attorneys went into a conference room to try and come to an agreement. They then talked to their clients and they couldn't come to an agreement. So they had to see the judge.

Just then the baliff opened the door for the parties to enter. He showed them where to sit. The witnesses were told to stay outside the courtroom until they were called. The parties were seated.

"All rise, The Honorable Judge Cone presiding"! Judge Cone entered the room. "You all may be seated." We are going on record v.ith this case for little Jalicia Ann Kennedy. If everyone is ready, will you please stand and raise your right hand for the oath. Baliff Hudson:" Do you all swear to tell the truth and nothing but the truth so help you God?" We do they all said in unison. Judge Cone stated: good we are on the record. She asked everyone to introduce themselves and to spell their names for the stenographer.

Well, lets begin: Donovan's attorney went first. He presented his witnesses which included Donovan's boss, who was his dad. They talked about how good of a man Donovan was and Donovan's dad was crying because he had not seen Donovan's new baby. But he knew he had to vouch for his son. Just then his attorney rested his case.

So, Ms. Coleman rose and presented their case. Which included Maschelle, Lisa, Joel, the videotape from Maschelle's mom.

As Lisa and Joel were seated outside the doors, they heard the elevator open. Entering in the courtroom is a very attractive lady. She says hello and sits a few seats down. Your honor, I would like to call my last witness to the stand. Ms. Samantha Thompson.

Inside the courtroom everyone's jaws dropped. The baliff opened the door. Ms. Samantha Thompson. The lady got up and entered the courtroom. Donovan screamed no way! Counselor Hardiman! The judge banged her gavel; Bam! Bam! Counselor Hardiman control your client before he is held in contempt of court. Mr. Hardiman calmed Donovan down while Samantha entered the courtroom and headed to the stand. Raise your right hand. Samantha was sworn in and Ms. Coleman began her questions. Your Honor we object and request a recess. For we were not prepared for this witness. Your Honor, Ms. Coleman said we object her name is on our witness list which was given prior to court. Mr. Hardiman, your objection is overruled. This witness is on the witness list, so Ms. Coleman can continue with her line of questioning. Your honor, if l may object, Ms. Thompson is married to the plantiff. No we are no longer married your

honor. I have the papers right here. Ms. Thompson showed the judge the papers. Everything seems to be in order. So Mr. Hardiman your objection is overruled, again. Donovan just sat there in disbelief as his ex—wife answered question after question. The court learned that Donovan was a "sperm donor." He was a horrible husband, that h e worked for his dad so he could get paid cash so he didn't have to pay child support and he doesn't see his kids. Judge Cone interrupted, Mr. Kennedy is all of this true? Your Honor, it's not like that at all! Then how is it exactly Mr. Kennedy? I want to take care of my kids and I do love them. However, I want to be able to take care of myself, as well. Ok, said Judge Cone. Continue Ms. Coleman. Your Honor we rest. Mr. Hardiman, any questions for this witness? No, your Honor we rest. Okay! I want to thank you all for coming today and presenting your cases. I would like to see Mr. Kennedy for a few questions in my chambers. We are at recess until 2:oo p.m. All rise! Baliff Hudson said as the Judge left the courtroom. Baliff Hudson directed everyone out of the courtroom; and directed Mr. Kennedy and the attorneys to the judge's chamber. He told the others to go to lunch.

Have a seat, Mr. Kennedy. Mr. Kennedy I want to ask you how do you plan to resolve these issues? I wanted to ask you these questions in chambers because I didn't want to seem like you were under pressure with all the accusations and things that were said. "So why should I give you joint custody of the child Jalicia? If you are not even doing right by your other children? What is so different with Jalicia? Your Honor she's the only one here in the city so its easier for me to see her. Ok. Mr. Kennedy. I'm willing to do something here for you. But, you will find that out when we return to court and if you don't agree with my decision at that time, then I want you to say it at that time so it can be on record. Thanks for your time; see you at 2 o'clock.

Lunch:

Maschelle, Joel and Lisa went to have lunch at the cotll'thouse diner. Maschelle called her mother to check on Jalicia and to let her know that it was gonna be a while longer and they were at recess until 2:oop.m. Her mother told her that everything was fine. Maschelle went back to join Joel and Lisa to finish lunch. Man, I wonder what the judge is talking to Donovan about? I don't even know why he's doing all this! "Probably, because you are happy"said Joel and Lisa in unison. Man, the things that Samantha stated in the courthouse were horrible. But, I guess I was blessed enough to only have his child and not be married to him. Lisa choked on

I Owe You Nothing

her water. Married to him! Is that who she is? His wife! Ex-wife, Maschelle ected. They also have 3 kids together. Wow! We were wondering who she was when we were at court. Well, it's 1:30 pm. I guess we better head back up. Okay. Joel paid the bill and gave Maschelle a big hug. It's all gonna work out for the best. Just think when its over you can focus on our wedding plans. "I guess you are right," Maschelle said.

Meanwhile back up on the 5th floor:

There was a knock on Judge Cone's door. Baliff Hudson stated Judge Cone, there are two people here to see you. Okay, Who are they? It's Ms. Thompson and Mr. Kennedy's father. They want to discuss some things with you before court resumes. Okay. Send them in. They entered into the judges chambers.

2:00 PM

All rise, Honorable Judge Cone presiding. Baliff will you invite all the witnesses and parties into the courtroom? Welcome witness and all interested parties in this case. I am shocked at some of the things that I have learned about Mr. Kennedy, in this matter. But I am also impressed by the people that came to visit me in chambers. I have to say that I wanted to totally deny your joint custody issue for Jalicia and send you to jail for just abusing the child support laws, as well as the court system. But that is not gonna help you become a man or a father to your children. Ms. Hernandez you are happy with your life. And I am happy for you. But I have to make a ruling in this matter. So here it goes: Donovan's father has paid child support for your daughter for six months in the amount of

$3,500 dollars. That's $583.00 dollars a month. Donovan has a previous obligation of $2,500.00 dollars a month for his other 3 kids. So I have to at least grant Mr. Kennedy visitation rights to Jalicia. Maschelle began to bawl. Ms. Coleman comforted her. It's okay Maschelle, lets hear the judge out first. It will be okay! The order will read that Mr. Kennedy will see your daughter every two weeks. This will allow you a break. But he has to furnish his own clothes, housing and all other needs for Jalicia. Mr.

Kennedy the other surprise for you is that you no longer work for your father. He has agreed to pay for your other children to come here and for you to take care of them, the whole summer, with no child support from Ms. Thompson. I want you to see what she goes through on her end of the situation. But, as a twist; remember I told you that if you disagree with my ruling; the time to speak up would be after I give my ruling and then you have to deal with the consequences, okay? You have a few months before your kids come and you must hold down a job. So, I'm willing to help you. I've called in a favor and you have to report to two interviews this week. One is at the Godspell Restaurant for a chef position. The other one is at the Cheesecake Factory, as a chef. The owners are expecting you. People have opened up and are willing to help you. Both jobs pay over $27.00 dollars an hour. You can either work both jobs and take care of yourself and your kids.

But you have to be willing to take these steps. On your childrens' return to Texas you must pay for their clothes, food and shelter while they are here. Pay for their plane tickets home; buy all their school clothes for the year and stay on top of your child support payments. Ms. Hernandez, it might seem unfair now but Jalicia is his daughter. And with the people that have stepped up hopefully, Mr. Kennedy will get his act and life together. But, your daughter can not miss out on him unless its his choice.

So, Mr. Kennedy what do you have to say. You are basically getting a fresh start. You get to make your own decision, the options have been presented. Your kids or not! What say you?

Donovan thought for a few minutes. Mr. Kennedy, Judge Cone said, "You have ten minutes to say yes or no." Donovan was mad at his dad for interfering. He told him that he hated him. His dad just got ready to walk out. But, before he left he said; "I have spoiled you for too long. I've been interfering, all this time and the one time you have to man up and stand on your own with everything handed to you. It is taking you forever to make such an obvious decision. Do You! I am so ashamed right now. I want to know all of my grandchildren so I'm gonna do my part to do that. I'm gonna be in their lives; instead of backing and supporting you, I should have just focused on them. Mr. Kennedy, time is up! What "'viii it be?

Judge Cone, my father is right and I asked for this situation in my life. So, I'm gonna(awkward silence) Man Up and take care of my kids. Thank you Mr. Kennedy. You have made a wise choice. I want to see you all back in a year. But, Ms. Hernandez and Ms. Thompson take my cards from my clerk, so if he doesn't hold up to his end of the bargain. Mr. Kennedy, you will face a year in jail for however many years it takes for all your kids to reach the tender age of And Jalicia is not even 3 months old, yet. So you might want to think about that. It is so ordered. Thank you all for coming. Have a great evening. All rise. Everyone left the courthouse.

. . . . 7 months later . . . .

"You are so beautiful!" Ann told her daughter. "You make a beautiful bride" she said holding, back tears. can not believe my baby is getting married. And you are marrying a great man. With tears running down her face, she ran out the room.

Lisa and Maschelle laughed, as she left. Then they both broke into tears simultaneously. The day is finally here! Girl, you got a God fearing man who loves you unconditionally. I'm praying thatI find one of his friends, for me.

I'm glad you didn't pick an ugly dress for me. They both laughed.

. . . . Wedding Scene . . . .

Pastor Thomas married them in Hawaii. Joel paid for everything. It was a beautiful ceremony with beautiful flowers and the ocean view. The honeymoon night was great because 9 months later I got a new little brother, Joel Anderson Jr.

"As for Donovan Kennedy, he turned out to be a great dad. I get to spend the summers with hi m and my other brothers and sister. My grandfather takes all of us ca mping every summer, as well. My dad is now co—owner of the family business and still works those two jobs to remind himself to always be a man and to Get Ove1•Himself and Be Willing To Take Care of Your Kids!" Just wanted to share a little passage of my diary.

Signed, Jalicia age17

SOMEBODY'S ALWAYS WILLING

WIL AND KIKI

Wil and Kiki attended Eudora High School in Eudora, Arkansas. Eudora is a small town in the southeast corner of Arkansas. It's 8 miles from the Louisiana line and 30 plus miles from Greenville, Mississippi. Eudora is a town where everybody knows everybody or at least who your family may be. Eudora reminds me of the town in the movie: The Fighting Temptations and also The Andy Griffith Show. There are loving and caring people, people striving to survive and people willing to help you. There are older people helping young people as well as, young people helping older people. You hear yes ma'am and no ma'am or yes sir and no sir everywhere. Kids can play in the streets safely. There are gardens, farms and people believe in working.

At Eudora High School, Wil was a junior and a star football player. Kiki was a sophomore and on the student council as a representative and on the yearbook staff. They were both in NJROTC together. Wil was being raised by a single mother who attended ever-y one of her son's games. They were reigning state champions and were s-o this year. Wil and his mother were so excited. His mother worked at the local garment factory. On the other hand, Kiki was being raised by her mother and her stepfather, a stepfather who was sexually abusing Kiki. That's why she was in so many activities so she could spend as much time away from home as she could. On weekends, if she was not at a fundraiser, Kiki would spend time with her grandmothers. One weekend, she would be with her maternal grandmother and the next weekend with her paternal grandmother. Her maternal grandmother knew what was going on but she couldn't take Kiki. or her brother and sister from the mother. Because her grandmother was getting up in age and the stepdad and mother kept saying "it wasn't true." So Kiki's books and school activities were her refuge. On the other hand Kiki's paternal grandmother never knew what was going on. The paternal grandmother moved to Arizona to be closer to her children.

It was Homecoming time at Eudora High School. Everyone was busy with floats, parade routines and the Homecoming Court. The Eudora Badger football team was yield with excitement because they were playing their rival team the Lakeside Beavers. Everyone was excited about who was gonna be on the Homecoming Court this year. Kiki didn't care. She knew she would be busy with one of her activities. Just then, the principal announced over the PA system The Homecoming Queen and her court. Kiki was happy because her neighbor Debbie was Homecoming Queen and the captain of the football team, Michael who was also the Student Council president was voted Homecoming King.

In ROTC class they told everyone to get their drill teams prepared and that the honor guard/color guard had to prepare for their Homecoming duties. Kiki was on the Honor Guard with Wil. So they practiced everyday in the gym with the Homecoming committee and the Homecoming Court. Wil and Kiki talked all the time anyway. They were so close. Wil would do the Honor Guard duties in the gym. But, his buddy Jesse would have to do it that night at the game; because Wil had to play football. After the game, of course there was gonna be a dance. Kiki never went to dances. But, this year something different happened. Wil asked Kiki to the Homecoming dance. As flattered as she was, she didn't know what to say. I'll answer you at practice this afternoon. Cool, said Wil. Kiki called her mom Kendra at lunchtime to ask her if she could go with Wil to the dance. Her mom said sure. Kiki was so excited she couldn't wait to see Wil at practice. At 4:00p.m. practice began and they went through everything. After practice

was over, Wil caught up with Kiki. She told him, yes she could go to the dance with him.

When Wil got home, his mom could see that he was excited about something. What's up? Why are you so happy? I asked Kiki to the Homecoming Dance; and she said yes she would go with me. Who's Kiki? Mom, you know Kiki.

I talk about her all the time. The girl with so much school spirit. You know Mr. Gant's step daughter, don't you? Yes.

"I think you could do much better than her. What about her neighbor, Debbie? She's pretty and plus I think something is going on over at Kiki's house. But, it's your choice." Oh mom, Kiki is cool. She's smart, funny, and shy. She's like the girl next door type. And plus, I figure she's always doing stuff on all those activities that for once, maybe she could enjoy her hard labor. Plus, I talk to her everyday because she is so easy to talk to. I can be myself around her." Okay, his mom said, but, can I at least meet her before the big day? "Sure, mom," said Wil.

When Kiki got home, it was another story. Her mom Kendra and stepdad, Frank were of course, arguing. He told Kendra that Kiki couldn't go. Kendra questioned him why not and it was on from there.

See, Kiki's stepfather wanted her, all to himself. That night the family sat together and had dinner. The kids took their baths and went to bed. Kiki's mom worked nights at the local gas station called Double Quick. So, the stepfather was always there with the kids. Around 2:00am that morning, her stepfather came into her room and raped Kiki. She screamed and cried and told him to stop! The more she screamed and resisted, the more things he did to her and also beat her. He told her: "This is all that boys/men

I Owe You Nothing

want from you. Your s.e.x. And I refuse to let them get it over me. You better not tell anybody, do you hear me? Or I will kill your sister and brother. You are gonna learn that you belong to me." After he was done; he left the room. Kiki laid there, crying. She was too scared to even move.

The next morning, Kiki woke up extra early. She wanted her mom to see her first thing that morning. She sat out on the porch waiting for her mom to come home. Kiki had a black eye and all types of scars. When Kendra got out the car and got onto the porch Kiki was there With her knees up to her chest.

She was there rocking and crying. Kiki's mom Kendra asked: "girl why are you out here especially this early in the morning? Kiki held her head up and her mom saw the black eye and bruises. "Kiki, what happened to you!" Kiki responded: "Mom, I don't want to live here anymore. I'm taking my stuff and moving out. Mom, he beat and raped me last night." He told me that all boys/men wanted from me was my s.e.x. And that if I told anyone he would kill Kiana and Khamal. I can't take this anymore. I want to live with grandma. I'm gonna move this afternoon after school.

Kendra said: "No, Kiki! We are gonna do this one together. I brought him into our lives to help out but he's been more of a burden. It's just that I love him. But, I love you guys more. I'm tired too. You are not going to school today. Kendra reached into her pocket and pulled out her cell phone. She called the police department. (4412). They were there in minutes. Kendra told them what happened. And told them she wanted him to be escorted off her premises. She told Frank that he would never hurt her or her family again." Kendra called h er job and told he1•boss that she would not be in that night and that she would explain the situation, later. She stated that she had a family emergency and she needed a few days off. Kendra had to take Kiki to the hospital. So she took Kiana and Khamal to her mom's house.

When they arrived at the hospital they rushed Kiki in and got her checked out. Kiki told them what happened. They told Kendra that Kiki had been penetrated. They arranged for her to spend the night for observation. They contacted child services so that they could talk to Kendra and Kiki. Kendra called the school to let them know that Kiki would be out for a few days. Child services sent a lady by the name of Ms. Arnold to talk to Kendra and Kiki. They both explained things to Ms. Arnold. She wrote notes as she listened. She told Kendra that she would need her permission to talk to her other children. Kendra told her that it was ok. By this time Kiki was sleeping. Ms. Arnold and Kendra went out in the hall to finish talking. Ms. Arnold asked Kendra what did she want to do and what her goals were? Kendra told Ms. Arnold that she needed a few days because she needed to focus on Kiki right now. Ms. Arnold told her that she understood and she left her card with Kendra. Kendra told her she would call but her main goal was to take care of her children first and foremost. Ms. Arnold and Kendra went back in to check on Kiki. Kendra told Ms. Arnold all Kiki wanted to do was go to Homecoming this year. And now she has to endure this turmoil. "I know one thing, if she still wants to go, I'm gonna make sure she does. I'm taking our lives back, she said tearfully. I can't believe I let the love of a man make me a donor to my kids. I just figured that if I worked and took care of them with food and clothes that they would be fine." Kendra was full of emotion. Now I'm here with my daughter, my baby, raped and beaten. Love Is Blind and it definitely, blinded me. I'm a single mother with 3 kids and their biological father is somewhere in Arizona. He thinks that just because he sends a check, that everything is cool. The ironic part is I have basically done the same thing. Except, I thought if I had a man in my life that it would be good. I guess I was wrong. I have short changed my children. I'm glad that they are very mannerable and not out of control. But, I think I know why Kiki is in so many activities. It's her escape from her reality. Ms. Arnold tried to calm Kendra. Just then Kiki woke up. "Mom, is everything ok?" "Yes, baby, sorry, I'm fine. How are you feeling?" "Okay, I guess," Kiki said. Ms. Arnold asked a few more questions and then she handed Kiki a card and told her to call her if she needed anything. Kiki and Kendra said goodbye to Ms. Arnold. Ms. Arnold told Kendra that it was late and that she would probably talk to Kiana and Khamal the next day at school or at their grandmothers.

That night over hospital dinner, Kiki and her mom talked. Kendra apologized and apologized. She told Kiki that things were gonna change from now on.

She asked Kiki if she still wanted to go to Homecoming. Kiki told her yes and that she was not gonna let what happened to her stop her from living

her life. Yes, I'm going to Homecoming and school. They talked until Kiki fell asleep.

.... The next day ....

Kiki and Kendra woke up and got prepared to leave. They both showered and Kiki laid back down. Just then the doctor entered the room. Dr. Russell told Kendra and Kiki that she should be discharged by noon. Kiki and Kendra were both pleased. He told them to put ice and cocoa butter on her eye. And he told Kiki that he was sorry that she had to go through that ordeal. And told her that she should always talk to a teacher, a counselor, police or tell someone as soon as something like that happens not only to her but anyone that she knew. He told her not to be afraid of anything. That it was their job to protect children like her from perverts like that. Kiki told Dr. Russell thank you. Dr. Russell told her "good luck."

.... Noon ....

The nurse ca me in with discharge papers and also a prescription for ibruprofen. She told her it was just in case she experienced any pain in the next few days. Kendra and Kiki left the hospital and went to Kendra's mom Ms. Luceal's house. Luceal gave them both great big hugs and told them she loved them. Oh, Kiki, look at your face. She hugged her again. "My poor baby." Kendra what are they gonna do to that bastard." They need to chop his dick off in torture and kill him where he stands. "Hell," I need to go down there and do it myself. Calm down mom, God and the courts are gonna handle Frank. God, you and I are gonna handle the kids. want them to continue to be on the right track. So, the decisions that we make now are critical. So, how will you be able to help if you are locked up. Mom, I need you now more than ever. Okay Kendra you, will. You know I'm gonna support my babies no matter what. "Thanks mom," Kendra said. They all had lunch there and then Kendra went to the school to pick up Kiana and Khamal from school, while Kiki took a nap at her grandmother's house. They arrived at the house and Kiana and Khamal jumped out the car and ran into the house. "Slow down, Where's Kiki they said in unison"? "She's asleep." We want to see her. You will. Just then Kiki walked out, Kiki, they said.

We miss you! We love you! They saw her eye and started crying. Oh, Kiki. Just then Kendra said we have to do the obvious. We need to go back home. Just then her mom said Kendra let's pray. Because you and your kids need to know that God is alive in this matter. And that we are family and what doesn't kill us will definitely make us stronger. All heads bowed:

"Prayer"

Father God we come to you as humbly as we know how. We thank you God for being in the midst of all this and the leader in all things. We pray for strength Lordfor the whole family. Touch right now Lord in the name of Jesus. We thank you for your Healing touch. Allowing Kiki to survive her ordeal. And to heal all of us after it. Show us how to encourage one another; and give us a strong mind Lord. We Love you Lord. We know that we may have tough times ahead Lord. But, we ask that you go ahead in the courts and in our lives and make the paths straight. Let your will be done. Lord we just thank you for you son Jesus. Protect us Father. These and other blessings we ask in thy darling son Jesus name. Amen. Amen. They all said. Ok, gang let's do this. They all left. They arrived home and it seemed different. Kiki walked in and started screaming and crying I'm free. Thank you Lord, I'm free. I'm no longer bound. She entered her room, she gave the sheets and everything to her mom so that she could give them to the police as evidence. Kiki was so happy. She remade her bed. Kendra was in the kitchen preparing dinner. Kiana and Khamal were doing homework.

Kiki asked her mom if she needed help and she said no. So, Kiki went and sat on the porch. She took the phone with her to call her friend Rhoshalonda to ask her what they did in school and if they had any homework. Rhoshalonda gave her the assignments. She also told Kiki that Wil had asked about her. Kiki blushed that was nice. Just then Ms. Arnold showed up so Kiki said that she had to get off the phone. Kiki let her in. How are you feeling child. I'm better, I'm taking it one day at a time. Kiki told her mom that Ms. Arnold was there. They invited her in. Dinner will be done soon. Would you like to stay. Ms. Arnold declined, actually I just came to talk to Kiana and Khamal. And also I have a surprise for Kiki. Kendra introduced Ms. Arnold to Kiana and Khamal. Ms. Arnold talked to them. Kiki went back to the porch. She sat there just enjoying the moment. She felt so relieved.

No arguing, it was quiet. It felt wonderful and she was enjoying her moment. Just then her neighbor Debbie came over. She wanted to talk to Kiki about Homecoming. She was so excited about being Homecoming Queen. She knocked and Kiki opened the door. Kiki what happened to you? Is this why you have not been to school? What's going on? Nothing. Kiki responded. Just some life changing things. What's up with you? I came to talk to you about Homecoming. You know about the dance right. Yes I do. Tell me you are going this time, Debbie said. Yes, I'm going. Do you have a date? Yes, I do. Debbie excitedly responded, really? Who? You never go anywhere. I know. But since I was asked, I decided to go. I'm going with Wil Jackson. Wow, he's a cutie. Yeah, he might not want to go after he sees this. Oh, it will be fine. Well, I'm gonna go. Just then Ms. Arnold came out. Kiki, I understand that Homecoming is coming up for you. And that you are going to attend. Yes ma'am, I am. Well I want to take some of the burden off of you for that. Kiki responded, what do you mean? Just then Kendra came onto the porch. Well, I have some friends and associates in high places. So, you are going in a limo. Here's the number, ask for Tom and tell him that you are the young lady I was talking about. Go to Greenville and you have a hair, nail and makeup appointment at the salon at the mall. And then go to Belk's in the mall and talk to the manager there. And you will find out that you have an original Baby Phat dress and accessories that was sent site to store for you.

Kiki just started crying. Oh thank you Ms. Arnold. Kendra, Kiana and Khamal and even Debbie were crying. Kiki gave Ms. Arnold a big hug and kept saying thank you. You are so very welcome. Ms. Arnold left and got in the car. The family was so happy.

Kiki was so excited. She couldn't wait for Homecoming and to tell Wil what was happening. The family had dinner and went to bed.

. . . . The next day . . . .

Kiki went to school bubbling. She couldn't wait to see Wil. Wil was waiJdng up the hall when he saw Kiki. Hey Kiki, what's up? I missed you at practice what's been going on with you/ hey what's wrong with your face? Kiki had forgotten about her eye with all the excitement going on. Oh, its nothing. Ok. If you need to talk or anything I'm here. Kiki said ok. Hey Wil, how about going to Homecoming in a limo? Wil was shocked, sure but how we gonna swing that? It's already work out. Homecoming is gonna be so much fun. I am so excited. Wil said me too. You know I asked about you while you were gone. Kiki responded:" yes I do." Rhoshalonda told me. I'll see you later at practice. They both smiled and left to go to class.

Later, that day after practice, Wil asked Kiki if he could walk her home. He had something to talk to her about. Kiki said sure. I just need to get a book out of my locker. I'll meet you outside by the ROTC building. As Kiki walked to her locker she wondered what Wil wanted to talk to her about. She thought maybe he didn't want to go to Homecoming with her anymore because of her face. Just as she closed her locker door, 'Wil said, Boo! Kiki jumped and said Wil, you are so silly. You play too much, let's go. As they walked they talked about school, sports, they asked about each others families. Then Wil asked the big question. Kiki, do you like me because I like you a lot. "Wow!" Kiki said. Sure, Will like you, I think you are a cool person and a great friend. Just a friend asked Wil. I guess, Kiki said I really don't know you except, from school. I mean I know this is a small town but ok, Wil stopped her in mid sentence. Well, why don't we try to get to know each other on a more personal note. Will you be my girlfriend? Kiki stopped walking. Are you serious? I would not have asked it If I wasn't. Wil, I would say yes but I have so much going on in my life right now. "I understand that," Wil responded. That's what I'm saying, I want to be the one that you share those things with. You don't have to go through it alone. "That's sweet," Kiki said. But, I would rather think about it first. You just wouldn't understand. They continued to walk in silence. Until they were about 2 blocks away from Kiki's house. "Stop Wil, they sat in the park on a bench. 'What's wrong Kiki? Well, I want to tell you what's going on with me. Then you can decide whether you want me as a girlfriend or not. Just don't bail out on me for Homecoming, deal? Deal, Wil agreed. And don't date me out of pity either. "Okay. "Okay. I won't." Wil stated.

Well, I am in all of the activities at school because I hated going home. Its my escape from the things that were going on at home. Which brings me to my face. I've been sexually abused for the last four years of my life by my stepfather. So, once I decided that I was going to Homecoming. My stepfather basically came into my room; raped and beat me and gave me a black eye. He told me that if he couldn't have me, no one could. He told me that all boys/men wanted from me was s.e.x. He threaten to kill my family. But, I was brave and told my mother that I was gonna move out. So she chose us and called the police and now, he is in jail. I went to the hospital. And was discharged the next day. But now Family Services is in our lives. Which is why Homecoming is so important. The social worker managed thru her friends to get me an original Baby Phat dress, an appointment for hair and makeup, and a limo. No one knows about my life so I pray that you will keep it between us. Kiki said with tears in her eyes. I never thought anyone would even be interested in getting to know me. That's my story. So, if you want to still date me, I would be honored; but I want you to take a few days and think about it. You can let me know at Homecoming. Will just took Kiki in his arms and just held her. Wow, Kiki that's a lot to take in but I will take the time to think about it and I will let you know. Wil took Kiki's hand and they walked hand and hand to Kiki's front door. Thanks for walking me home and also for listening. You are welcome. I'm sorry that you had to go through that situation. But, things can only get better now. Hey Wil, call me when you get home. Kiki wrote her number down and handed it to him.

"Sure, no problem, Wil said. Wil walked home smiling. He unlocked the door. His mother, Sharon looked at her son smiling and asked: "What are you so happy about?" Oh, nothing mom. I just walked Kiki home and we had a very nice discussion. I even told her how much I really liked her and asked her to be my girlfriend. Wow, that is something to be happy about. Sharon said to her son. Are you sure? I mean I'm happy with whatever makes you happy. But, I've told you that I think something is going on at that home. "Mom, stop! I'm sure shes the girl for me." "Hey let's go to Greenville so I can pick out my suit for Homecoming, Wil said. Sure, we can go as soon as you finish your homework, mister. "Yes ma'am," Wil said and gave his mother a kiss on the cheek as he ran to his room. One hour later, he returned. Mom, I'm done with my homework. Are you ready to go? Yes, I am. I'll be right there. They got in the car and headed toward Greenville, Mississippi.

Where do you want to go and find a suit? How about "Looking Good". They usually have nice suits and have them on sale. Well, "Looking Good", here we come. So, you can make my son look good! She laughed. Oh, mom, you are so funny. They made it and looked around. They picked out a nice suit and shoes. Just as they opened the door to leave, they bumped into Debbie. Hi, Debbie, excuse me. I didn't sec you there. Hi, Wil, Debbie responded. What has you here? "Homecoming shopping?", she asked. Yes, said Wil and I assume you are doing the same. Yes, you know the Queen has to look good. Sharon cleared her throat. Oh, I'm son-y mom. Debbie this is my mom. Ms. Sharon Manley. Hello Ms. Manley its nice to meet you. You have a very nice son. I try to raise him right. You seem like a nice, young lady yourself, Debbie. Why thank you.

Wil aren't you excited for Kiki and the stuff that lady got her. I don't know who the lady is but Kiki is gonna be the talk of Homecoming with that original Baby Phat dress and the limo. Sharon's eyes got big, limo? What limo? "It's nothing mom, everything's taken care of," he said while giving Debbie the eye to be quiet. Yes, its gonna be a blast! Anyway, I will see you at school tomorrow Debbie. Come on mom, let's go! Let's get to Checker's before they close. They left and drove the rest of the way home in silence. They arrived home. Thanks mom for taking me and buying

I OWE YOU NOTHING

my Homecoming stuff. You're welcome, son. They ate their food, bathe and went to bed.

The next day, Kiki made it to school. Wil ran up to her and apologized for not calling her when he got home. Oh, it's okay. I had a lot of homework to do anyway. "No," Wil said:" I want to explain!" I went shopping with my mom last night for Homecoming. We also ran into Debbie over there. I just want you to know that I thought about you all night. It was late when we returned and I did not want to disrespect your house by calling that time of night. "It's okay,"

Kiki said. "Hey, are you ready for the final practice today? "I sure am" Wil said. I'm hyped about the game and the dance. "So am I," said Kiki. The big day is tomorrow. I know Kiki, said. I have to practice with ROTC, then help out with the float. And then go to Greenville to get everything tonight. So I will see you later at practice. "See you there," Wil said and surprisingly gave Kiki a kiss on her cheek, as he ran off to class. Kiki just stood there with her hand on her cheek in amazement. She headed into her English class gleaming. Ms.

Ford's class was one of Kiki's favorite. She really cared about her students and was very smart and helpful. Kiki smiled and spoke and rushed to her seat. She quickly jotted down a note and handed it to her friend Rhoshalonda. It read, "Wil kissed me." He asked me to be his girlfriend. Rhoshalonda handed the note back and asked: What did you say?" "Attention class", Ms. Ford stated.

I'll tell you later Kiki whispered. "Okay," Rhoshalonda responded. They discussed Beowulf in class that day. The bell rang and Ms. Ford announced to them that school would be ending at noon tomorrow so that everyone could prepare for Homecoming. Kiki was happy to hear that. When class was over, Kiki told Rhoshalonda that she told Wil to think about it for a few days to be sure and he could give her the answer before Homecoming. Just then Debbie and Michael walked up. "Hey guys, What's up? "Nothing much" Kiki and Rho replied. Are you excited that school's out early tomorrow? Yes, everyone agreed. Debbie asked Kiki if she wanted to go to Greenville with her to get the things done that she needed. Kiki said: "sure". We have practice and then I have to help with the Student Council float. "Aren't you helping Michael?" Kiki, asked. Of course, but we should be done with everything by 6:00p.m. So, we can go after that. I just have to check with my mom, first. She wanted to be the one to take me so she can approve everything. I will just have her and my grandmother meet us there.

Practice was great! Kiki and Wil said their goodbyes and Kiki went to meet Michael and the rest of the Student Council to finish their work on the float. They worked so hard, until it was finished. The float was a Badger and a Beaver fighting over a football, with a goal post and players scrambling for the ball. Ivan helped with the engineering of the moving players and animals. It was now 6:00p.m. and Debbie was pulling up in her mom's car. "Are you ready?" Sure, let's go. Michael asked; is there room for one more? "Sure", Debbie said. "Do you need to get something from over there?" "Yes" Michael said. "Okay" said Debbie because I can not have you looking like a bum tomorrow." They all chuckled. The ride over to Greenville was cool. They got to the "Y" and Michael asked Kiki who was she going to Homecoming with and she told him Wil Jackson. So he said: "cool". At least you are finally coming to something. I was wondering? Well, we were wondering if you had room in that limo that you are getting? And if so, if Debbie and I could ride with you and Wil. Kiki said: "that she would think about it and would ask WU if he was comfortable with that." "What do you mean you have to ask Wil? It's your limo," Debbie said. Just as they were crossed the bridge Michael hit Kiki in the head. What was that for? Because we are the King and Queen of Homecoming and we should be in a limo. Who do you think you are? Or do you think you are better than everyone else? Debbie pulled the car into a wooded trail off the road behind Shipley's Donuts. Kiki asked why did she do that? Just then Michael pulled out a gun. Debbie panicked; "this is not what we discussed Michael you are taking this too far". No, this bitch is gonna let us ride with her or she won't make it out of these woods. Kiki kept pleading, no please Michael don't do this! Just then Debbie grabbed for the gun and Michael snatched it back and hit Debbie in the head and knocked her unconsious. He asked K.iki again and she said: "no," I'm not afraid of you. I've been through too much and I'm not gonna" Pow!"

I Owe You Nothing

Michael shot the gun in the air. Finish that sentence and you are done for. As a matter of fact, let me show you what Wil is gonna want tomorrow night. Michael jumped on top of Kiki and began raping her. This is what Wll is gonna want from you. K.iki was screaming and crying but no one heard her. Oh, by the way my Dad said to tell you hi, his "little sweet thang". K.iki was confused but she couldn't say anything because Michael had his hand around her throat, choking her. He kept talking, see Frank Gant is my father and he told me to make sure you didn't make it to Homecoming. He also told me how good your s.e.x was and that if he couldn't have you, then should. Will is a punk and you belong to me now. K.iki couldn't believe what she was enduring! She blacked out praying, asking God why was she going through this in her life.

Michael in the meantime had thrown her out the car alongside Debbie who was still knocked out, too. He took the car back to Arkansas and parked it at Debbie's house and knocked on the door and gave Debbie's mom the keys.

He told her that they had all gone to Greenville and that Debbie was with Kiki and her family. He also said that Debbie had asked him to drive the car back since she was gonna stay and continue shopping and getting ready for Homecoming. Debbie's mom said thanks and Michael walked away laughing like nothing happened.

About an hour, later Kiki's mom made it to Belks. That's where they agreed to meet. So Kendra went to the counter to ask for the manager. The manager came and Kendra told her that she was Kiki's mom and was wondering if she had come to pick up the dress, already. The manager told her no, that the dress was still there. Kendra wondered, well I was suppose to meet her here at 7:30p.m. and it's now 8pm. I know she has a hair and makeup appointment, so maybe she went there first so she can get that part over with. The store manager asked Kendra if she wanted to take the dress. She told her if she could verify the information that she would give her the dress because they were closing at 10 o'clock and she didn't want Kiki to miss getting the dress. So Kendra took the dress and fow1d her mom who was looking at pantsuits. Oh this dress is so beautiful. Kiki is gonna love this and she sent matching shoes. We are gonna have to definitely thank Ms. Arnold for this. This is too much!

Ms. Luceal(Kiki's grandmother) paid for the items she picked. She, Kendra and the kids went on their way to the salon in the mall. Just then, Kendra's stomach started hurting like she was nervous about something. Kiana said, Mom are you okay? Yes, she stated. They made it to the salon to see if Kiki was there and the receptionist stated that Kiki had not been there and that Ms. Tawanna was getting frustrated because she was the one who was doing Kiki's hair, nails and makeup. Kendra didn't understand. So, she took out her cellphone and called Debbie's mom Diana. Hello Diana, how are you? This is Kendra, Kiki's mom. Oh, hello Kendra, how's the shopping going? Tell my daughter that she could have called to let me know she was letting Michael drive the car home. Kendra's mouth dropped. What do you mean? Your daughter is not with me. I was calling to see if you have heard from the girls; and I didn't know that Michael anybody was going? Whose this Michael person? Diana said "you know," Mary's son that lives down the street. He brought my car back about 15 minutes Ago and said that Debbie was with you and your family. She's not? No, I'm looking for Kiki, as well. Just then Kendra got another pain in her stomach. Something's wrong, Kendra said. Kendra apologized to Ms. Tawanna about her daughter's lateness and she told Diana to call Mary and ask Michael again about the girls. Kendra hung up and called the police and told them about the missing girls. Diana called Mary and Michael answered the phone. Michael, this is Ms. Diana, Debbie's mom. where is she? Kendra just called and said that the girls are not with her. 'Where are they? Michael just hung up the phone. He laughed. His mom asked who was he talking to and he said i t was someone with the wrong number. So Mary went back to preparing dinner. The police made it to the mall and Kendra, Ms. Luceal, Kiana and Kha mal met them in the security office of the mall. They were looking over tapes to see if the girls were seen on any cameras entering or exiting the mall. Nothing showed up on the tapes. The police gathered all the information and told Kendra that it was best if she took her family home. But Kendra said:" no." She told her mother to just take the children home and that she would stay in Greenville and

I Owe You Nothing

would be home as soon as she heard anything. I just can't believe Kiki did not show up. She was so excited about Homecoming.

Diana kept calling but there was no answer. So she walked to Mary's house. She knocked on the door and waited. Mary came to the door and said hello Diana, how are you? I'm confused, your son Michael brought my car to me tonight and said that Debbie asked him to drive it back from Greenville and that she was with Kendra and her family shopping. I've been calling, I asked Michael where the girls were and he hung up. So I've been calling and no one answered. So I decided to come over. "Well, come on in," Mary told Diana and we will get to the bottom of this. Michael came from his room. Hey mom, whose at the door? Michael's eyes got big as baseballs and he took off out the backdoor with the ladies running behind him. Michael, stop, we just want to talk to you. Michael, Mary called but he couldn't hear her. He was too far gone. So Mary and Diana came back in the house where Mary called the police. Chief Webster and Sgt. Gaston came to the house. The ladies explained what was going on. In all the commotion, Diana had forgotten to call Debbie's cell. Just then, she called. The phone just rang. She called again nothing. The third time she called Debbie answered and said "HELP" and passed back out. Debbie, Debbie, where are you? Debbie answer me, where are you?! Her screams were not answered. Chief Webster said just don't hang up? We can track the signal. We are gonna call the Greenville police to let them know what's going on, just in case the girls are over there.

Diana called Kendra's phone from Mary's house phone. Kendra! Kendra! Something's wrong! Debbie answered but she won't say anything now. I'm calling from Mary's phone Chief Webster and Sgt. Gaston are tracking the phone signal. Kendra let the Greenville officers know and dispatch was talking to them at the same time. Just then, Officer Watkins walked into Mary's house. We have not found your son, yet. But the tracking system from the phone shows the girls are in Mississippi. There's a wooded trail right off E.Reed Rd. The Greenville police are there now combing the area and Ms. Kendra is there with them. Good! Let's just keep your phone on until they dispatch me back all clear. Officer Harris is out searching for Michael with Officers Gayfield and Johnson. The Chief and Sgt. Gaston are in Greenville helping with the search and to also bring Ms. Kendra home, if she needs it. Diana called Kendra again as Mary made coffee and tea for them. Kendra, where are you? Diana asked. I'm on E. Reed Rd with the officers. This is some very scary stuff Diana, I have to tell you. I'm sitting in this police car and I can't do anything. Knowing that something might be wrong is just too much. Have you been able to talk to Michael?

No, he ran out of the house but the police officers are looking for him. Someone's beeping in on Mary's phone. I'll call you later.

Mary your phone is beeping. Maybe its Michael! Hello, Michael? No Mary this is Sharon Manley, how are you? Confused to say the least, what's going on'!Well your son Michael is here. What? Great! Is he o.k.? Actually he has a gun in his hand and is asking for my son. I called the police and they are sending someone over. What is going on? He's screaming that he wants to talk to Wil. But I made Wil stay in his room. Does this have something to do with why you are confused? "Yes," said Mary. My son is probably in trouble and I don't know why. Just then the police had Sharon's house surrounded.

Drop your weapon Michael! No, not until I talk to Wil. Wil opened the door to his room. Mom, let me talk to him. Maybe, I can help. No! Sharon screamed! He has a gun! Let the police handle this. What is this about Wil? I have no idea, mom. I've been home since Homecoming practice was over. Drop your weapon, son! Will Michael screamed. You wanna know where she is? "Who is she?" Sharon asked. "I have no idea", Wil said. Ok you talk to him through the door. Do not open i t at anytime! Officers, 'just let me say what I gotta say and I'll drop my weapon." That bitch thinks she's better than everyone else You know, Kiki. What! What have you done with Kiki? Where is she Wil screamed: She better not be hurt! Not only is she hurt she has been raped by me, too. That bitch and her friend Debbie are in Greenville hurt and left for dead. Kiki has destroyed my life for the last time! What are you talking about! All she had to do was let me ride in that limo with yall! Especially since my dad is the reason she is even getting it! What do you mean? Sharon asked

Mary what does he mean by that! She's explaining everything that's going on with Michael at this time. Oh, no! He didn't say that did he? Mary what is going on? Diana chimes i n; who is it Mary? Is it Michael? What's he saying? What's going on? Tell Wil to ask him where the girls are in Greenville. Wil asked him and Michael just laughed. "I hope they are dead, Michael said!" She took my dad from me! I had to show her that she can't just destroy people's lives! It's hard living down the street watching your dad with another family! And then coming over to your house to screw your mom!

Ok, Mary what is h e talking about! Mary started crying, tell Michael to put his gun down; tell him it's not Kiki's fault. It's Mine! Sharon and Wil told Michael what his mom said. Man, put the dam gun down! "'Where is Kiki," Wil asked. Michael just laughed. •what's so funny? You know what Michael said.

Someone is always willing to love, help, save, cherish, hurt or do what they will with you. My dad is Frank Gant and I have lived right down the street from him and Kiki's mom all these years. I'm the one that first put it in my dad's head how fine guys thought Kiki was. And he wanted her ever since. As long as he could have her, he was happy. Now he's in jail because that bitch finally said something and her dumb ass mom finally took a stand! So, he told me to make sure she didn't get to go to Homecoming! "So, guess what, she's not going". I've never had him as a dad because he chose her bitch ass mom over my mom, who was his wife! The ultimate donor betrayal!

(Help take care of other kids and ignore yours that live right down the street). If she makes it, tell the bitch I will see her in hell! Pow! Pow! Gunshots. Sharon, Sharon what happened? Sharon dropped the phone. Wil, Wil Help Me! Help Me! The police burst through the door!Wow!Homicide/ Suicide situation. 1st pow Michael had shot through the door where Wil was standing. 2nd pow Michael had killed himself. The ambulance came, the coroner came. The ambulance rushed Wil and his mom to Chicot Memorial Hospital. Mary just stood there in shock. Officer Watkins was dispatched and told what had transpired. He told Diana and Mary what happened. He offered to take Mary to the coroner's office. No, not until I find out what is going on with those girls. My son's dead now. There's no helping him.

Just then she remembered something. She told Officer Watkins and Diana about a park that Michael and Frank use to go to when they lived in Greenville.

And that there was a bike trail that Michael loved. It was the only part of that park that was left before they built the little strip mall where Shipley

Donuts is located. She told them to go there. You will probably find them in a field of mixed irises. He use to call it Mom's bouquet because when I married Frank I carried irises. Diana grabbed Mary's phone and called Kendra. Officer Watkins dispatched through to Chief Webster who explained to the other officers what was said. Chief Terry of the Greenville police said:" I know exactly where that area is located." The officers came back toward the police cars and headed to the left, toward Shipley's. Kendra watched and not five minutes later the officers came out with the girls in their arms headed toward the ambulance.

Kendra is allowed to come out the car to verify that they were the girls. They were then rushed to Delta Regional Medical Center.

2 weeks later

Debbie and Kiki arc released from the hospital. They return home. Debbie had suffered a concussion, but was doing a lot better. Kiki had suffered a concussion, a broken rib from the struggle and vaginal tearing. Wil suffered a gunshot wound to the neck. It just missed his juggler. After ten hours of surgery and a week in the hospital, he was fine.

The students at Eudora High School missed them a lot. They returned to school three weeks later. Ms. Mary(Michael's mother) helped the school throw another Homecoming dance in Wil, Kiki, and Debbie's honor. Debbie was given her Homecoming Queen crown. Debbie, Kiki and Wil were best friends from then until now.

Seven years later, after college and landing their dream jobs. Kiki and Wil got married and had 2 beautiful children. They named their son Michael to remind them to remain real parents to always love each other. Debbie was not charged because the plot changed and because she had suffered in the ordeal too. Kiki was able to forgive her. Debbie is also the proud god mother to Kiki and Wil's two beautiful children.

As for Diana, Kendra and Mary they realized as single parents, you have to stick together. Mary told Kendra about how she was married to Frank and how he had left her and her son. Then, that Frank had helped them move to Eudora and told them where to move and everything. Mary told Kendra how he made her and Michael live that close to him. Mary also told Kendra how she was sorry for what happened. Kendra was able to forgive Mary, and Mary forgave Kendra Kendra never knew any of this, until Mary told her.

As for Mr. Frank Gant, well you know Momma Knows Best. And the fact that Someone's Always Willing. Frank's dick was chopped off and he was killed as he stood in prison.

As for Ms. Arnold, the social worker from Family Services, well I'm the one telling the story. Kendra keeps in contact with me monthly. She thanks me for helping her and her family. I love small communities and towns.

Because Someone's Always Willing!

Somebody Prayed For Me

Victor and Junise

Victor was an African American, 6 feet tall and weighed 180 pounds. Junise was Italian and African American female, 5 feet 7inches tall and weighed 140 pounds. She was Italian on her dad's side and African American on her mother's. They were a lovely couple. They were high school sweethearts at Harding High School in St. Paul, Minnesota. They were the Valedictorian and Salutatorian of their class, respectively. They both left Minnesota and attended Philander Smith College in Little Rock, Arkansas. They agreed they wanted to go south because it was warmer there. They wanted to experience something different than Minnesota. They attended Philander for four years, graduating Cum Laude and Magna Cum Laude of their class, respectively. They both received their masters degrees from Harding University in Searcy Arkansas Victor's degree was in architecture and Junise's in Nursing. After graduating school, they moved back to Minnesota and began working in their fields. Six months later, Victor asked Junise to marry him. She said yes and they were married the following June and spent their honeymoon in Las Vegas. Junise got pregnant on their honeymoon and their daughter Tammy was born. Two years later they were blessed with twins: Zandara and Zachary. They had a great life together; they we1•e living the American Dream.

Victor worked for Williams, Turner and Martin archltectural firm and Junise worked at Children's Hospital. They worked hard everyday.

5 years later

Victor is now the head architect at his company and Junise is the charge nurse of her tmit. Tammy is 8 and the twins are 5 and a half years old. They had their dream home built in the frogtown area of St. Paul, Minnesota, designed by Victor.

It had 5 bedrooms, 3 bathrooms, a 3 car garage and 2 offices.(One for each of them). It also had a large basement with an activities room for the kids. It was a lovely home on the outside. But, what was it like inside the home? Junise's Aunt Mae came to live with them. She was only ten years older than Junise. But she had nowhere else to go; so she lived with them and helped out with the kids. She was a big help. She had been the owner of her own candle shop but it gone bankrupt. The family always wondered why.

One day, Aunt Mae noticed a change in Junise. "Are you okay sweetie?" Aunt Mae asked Junise. "Yes, Aunt Mae I'm fine", Junise responded. Junise grabbed her purse and went into the bathroom. Aunt Mae waited for her to come out. "Okay, Junise don't lie to me; something is 'Wrong with you. Are you pregnant", asked Aunt Mae. Junise replied, "No, Aunt Mae I'm not pregnant and everything is fine." As Junise started to prepare dinner, she turned up the radio and was just whistling and preparing dinner. She was dancing around like nothing was wrong at all. Aunt Mae went to the activity room to play with the twins and to help Tammy with her multiplication tables. It was brought up at a parent teacher conference that Tammy had been having trouble with them.

Victor came home around 6:oop.m. He noticed that Junise was dancing around the kitchen and started dancing behind her. He moved every time she moved. Then he kissed her on her neck. Victor! What are you doing? You startled me! She then turned and gave him a hug and kiss. He asked, What's for dinner? She said:" I'm making pork chops, rice, gravy and biscuits. Don't you see the pork chops in the skillet?" He said," Baby, there is nothing in the skillet. "Yes, there is!" she said and looked in the skillet and there was nothing there. She looked in the fridge and realized she had not taken the pork chops out of the freezer. Victor said: Oh, its okay baby, we can order from the Chinese restaurant, down the street. Jw1ise was so embarrased. She just ran back to the bathroom. Just then Aunt Mae came from the activity room. "Oh, hi Victor, I sec you are home. May I speak to you for a minute?" Sure, they went into the living room. "Victor, have you noticed a change in Niecey? No, I haven't; she's probably just tired. You know she works a lot. Maybe she needs a vacation." "No," Aunt Mae said. "I think it's deeper than that. She's been in that kitchen dancing for about an hour or so and has not even boiled water." Victor chuckled. Well, we will keep a close eye on her. I have to order dinner now so we will be able to eat something, soon. He took out his cellphone and called New Asia restaurant to order food for the family. He knew it was Junise's favorite restaurant to Order from. Once the food arrived they all sat and ate talking over the events of the day. Just then Junise excused herself from the table and went back to the bathroom. Upon her return, she was happy and dancing again. "Are you sure you are okay sweetie?" "Oh, Aunt Mae I am fine. Just happy to be around my family." She kissed Tammy, Zachary and Zandara and spun around the room as if she was in top flight. The kids burst into laughter. After dinner, Victor cleared the dishes, helped Aunt Mae put the kids to bed. Junise was still dancing around the house not even noticing what was going on around her. Everyone eventually went to bed. Victor started to talk to Junise but she was knocked out. Victor said to himself," I guess she's tired from all that dancing. I will just talk to her in the morning.

. . . . The next morning . . . .

Victor woke up early. He wanted to catch Niecey before she went to work to make sure she was ok. But she was already up. Or so he thought. He put on his slippers and robe and went downstairs to see if she was there. But she wasn't. Man, it's 5:45a.m. in the morning, where is she? He went into the kids room to sec if maybe she was laying in one of their rooms. But, she wasn't.

He didn't want to wake Aunt Mae because he knew Junise wouldn't be in there. And he knew Aunt Mae would be getting up soon to prepare breakfast and to begin her praise and worship which she did every morning.

He would get up early just to listen sometimes. He just kept feeling like something was wrong. He called the cellphone, no answer. He called the OnStar in her vehicle, no answer. He called her job to see if she was there and they stated, no. So, he asked to speak to her friend, Cindy. Oh, Victor she's not due in until about 8. Is everything okay? It's kind of early for you to be looking for her. I'll have her call you when she makes it in, okay? "Thanks Cindy," Victor said. About 6:15a.m. Victor heard Aunt Mae doing her praise and worship service. He just sat there and listened. He was praying silently for the safe return of his wife. Aunt Mae eventually came out of her room to prepare breakfast. She got into the living room, where Victor was still praying. She waited until he was finished. "Good morning, Victor", how are things with you this morning? "Not so good," said Victor. Niecey is missing today. I woke up early to talk to her about last night. But, when I got up at 5:45a.m. this morning, she was gone. She's not answering her cell, On-Star, she's not at work or anything. Her friend Cindy said that she is suppose to be at work at 8 am so I'm just trying to wait until then. Well, come on in the kitchen; I'll make some coffee while I make breakfast and we can wait together. Victor agreed but he decided to get the kids up for breakfast and school. Victor got the kids dressed and got them ready for school. By the time the kids were done eating, it was 8 o'clock. Aunt Mae said that she would take the kids to the bus stop and then he can make the call. The kids attended Crossroads Elementary School, an all year round school. Aunt Mae got the kids onto the bus and then returned into the house. Victor grabbed the phone and called Junise's job, again. This time her friend Cindy answered because she knew Victor would be calling. Good morning Children's Hospital nursing station 3rd floor Pediatrics, this is Cindy, How may I direct your call? Hello Cindy, this is Victor did Junise show up, yet? "No, Victor unfortunately she did not. She did not call or show up today. And its not like her to be late." "Okay Cindy, thanks". You're welcome. Call me if you find out anything. Victor decided to call the police. He also called his job to let them know that he wouldn't be in the office today. He told them he would just work from home.

When Victor called the police to report his wife missing. They said they would send someone to the house but for Victor to know that they really could not begin looking for Junise until she was missing at least 24 hours. Victor hung up the phone and waited for the police to arrive. "What happened?" Aunt Mae asked. "She did not go to work and the police are on their way here to ask questions." Wow! I hope nothing bad has happened to her. You and I both said Victor. Seven minutes later the police arrived at the house. Victor welcomed the detectives into the house. They asked question after question. Victor and Aunt Mae answered the questions to the best of their knowledge They even asked if she had clothes missing? If she had left any clues to where she might be? They both answered "no." But stated that they would check around and keep their eyes opened for anything. The detectives thanked them for answering their questions and stated that they had all the information they needed and handed Victor and Aunt Mae their cards. Just in case they needed to use them. The detectives were escorted out and thanked for coming. Aunt Mae told Victor not to worry that everything would be fine. She told him that God knows all and sees all. Victor thanked Aunt Mae and said he needed to hear that. Aunt Mae asked: "Do you want anymore coffee or can I get you something to eat? You hardly touched your breakfast.""No thanks," Victor said. "I'm gonna look around to see if Junise left a note or some type of clue to where she might be. I can not even focus on work right now, maybe I will be later." Aunt Mae told him that she would help upstairs. They both began looking for something that would lead to finding Niecey. An hour into looking, Victor came from the kids activity room with an envelope in his hand. Aunt Mae! Aunt Mae! Is this your envelope? She examined it and said, "no Victor its yours". Your name is written on it and its Niecey's hand" Titing. Victor was just happy to see something at this point. He opened the letter and began reading. The letter said;

Dear Victor,

I have been wanting to tell you this for years now. I just didn't know how to tell you face to face. You know that I love you and the kids with all my heart. But, Im addicted to crystal meth. I have been using since I started working at the hospital. U could have been that everything happened so fast after graduating. Or it could have just been o lot of pressure, period. Well, I thought about the events that occurred last night and I have decided that I'm no longer fit for a family. The drugs are starting to affect my home life and family. So it's time to move on. You and Aunt Mae con handle the kids. Will you tell them that I LOVE THEM everyday and that this is not their fault'. I hope that I will kick this habit. Will you both just keep me in your prayers? Sorry, I left the way that I did but it's for the best. Victor angrily threw the letter across the room, without even finish reading it. Crystal meth? What? How did this happen? Was I that blind not to notice the changes? What am I gonna do? I Love Her! I said vows before God that said: "for better or for worse." And she didn't, couldn't even talk to me about this. We could have gotten her some help, Rehab, Therapy, whatever It took We Are A Family First! Aunt Mae took Victor's hand; Victor, let it out, go ahead. You need to get all of your frustrations out now because you and God have three kids to raise, and the kids do not need to see you like this!

You are the parent now! God has Niecey! You are gonna have to be strong for them. We don't know how long its gonna take but He's Always On Time.

Victor broke down in tears and cried for about two hours. Aunt Mae called detectives Boone and McKinney back to let them know about the letter that was found. They thanked her for the information and reminded her that the process couldn't start until she was missing for 24 hours. She thanked them and hung up the phone.

I Owe You Nothing

Aunt Mae starting preparing for the kids return home from school. She was preparing fruits and vegetables for their afternoon snacks and had taken food out for dinner. Victor had fallen asleep on the couch. So Aunt Mae just kept doing what she was doing. About an hour later, Victor woke up and came to the kitchen where Aunt Mae was preparing food. "What time is it," he asked. Oh, its 2:00pm. Sorry Aunt Mae for breaking down earlier this is just so overwhelming. How am I suppose to do all this? What am I suppose to tell our children? I still have to call Kevin and Veronica (Junise parents) and let them know what's going on; and to see if Niecey has called them or anything. Okay, I can give Kevin and Veronica a call. She called and Kevin said that they would be there in thirty minutes because Veronica was in with the doctor and that he would let her know and they would be over. Veronica had been diagnosed with breast cancer. By the time Niecey's parents got there the children were home from school. "NaNa and PopPop the kids said in unisom. "What are you doing here?" "Can I get a hug?" Victor asked the kids.

"Daddy! You're home early," said Tammy. "Yeah, I worked from home today."

Kids let's go to the activity room so we can let your Dad talk to NaNa and Pop Pop. Your snack is down there. You guys can come up when you are done with your snacks and Tammy's done with her homework. I'm sure NaNa and PopPop will not leave without hanging out with you all. "You promise? Asked Zandara and Zachary. "We promise". Veronica and Kevin said. Okay. I will be back shortly said Aunt Mae so we can all figure this out. Victor said take your time Aunt Mae. I'm gonna wait a few more minutes on Cindy. She wanted to know what the outcome of the days events were so, I've called her to come over as well, and she should be on her way. "Okay." Aunt Mae responded. As Aunt Mae left the room with the kids, Victor showed Niecey's letter to her parents. I couldn't finish reading it because I was so upset at how selfish she is being. Just then the doorbell rung. Victor opened the door and it was Cindy so he invited her in the house. So, did you find out anything? Yes, Junise left a note in the activity room and the police will start looking for her tomorrow if she doesn't show up in the required 24 hour time frame. Cindy and Victor entered the living room where Kevin and Veronica were standing. Wow! "Victor" Kevin said: We will support you in any decision you make and help with the kids, of course. Veronica was crying, oh, it ok. Mom; Victor said. Oh I feel like I might have added the extra stress with my cancer. "No," Victor said. "We can not blame ourselves, the kids or anything else. This is all Niecey" "You are right Victor I'm just sorry the way this has all came out in the open like this. Well, I guess at work whatever happens will happen. She will probably be let go if she doesn't show or call in two days. But, Victor if you need help with anything, definitely feel free to give me a call. I have to go before Ray sends out an APB for me. It was good to see you both Kevin and Veronica she said. Catch you guys later; Cindy said. "Thanks for all your help Cindy", Victor said and I will keep you posted. Cindy added:" I will keep you all in my prayers. Good night."

Just then Mae was coming from the activity room. Kevin charged her: "Mae, you did this, didn't you!" I knew when you moved in here . . . .

"What?! I would never do that." I've been clean for the last seven years. You know years of completion and I Thank God everyday for saving me from my addiction; But, I will not be accused of this! I knew those signs were there but I didn't want to believe it and she said that everything was fine. I knew! I knew! I'm sorry for what has happened but I can assure you I had nothing at all to do with this," said Aunt Mae. Victor is standing there with his mouth wide open. He turns his head and said: "What are you all talking about? Will somebody tell me what's going on?" "Hello, I'm having household issues here! Sit down Victor," Aunt Mae said. So he sat on the sofa and Aunt Mae told him the real reason she lost her business was because she had a heroin addiction, years ago; and that she has been sober for seven years now and enjoyed watching their kids and helping out. She told him how she was into church, now; and she and God had completely turned her life around. "Whatever," Ke" in said. "Once a junkie always a junkie." "Victor, don't you believe that; If God can do it for me he can do it for anybody," said Aunt Mae.

Kevin, I could say that you may be right; but, I hope and pray that it is not true in this case because I feel that with prayer, God and us together will help the junkie in front of us now and that once she's sober she will stay that way. For the sake of her family, especially, her kids. Veronica chimed in, "Mae is right, we can't start pointing fingers now; we have to stand united for these children and Victor. "Victor!Victor!" Veronica asked," Are you okay? Yeah, Yeah. I'm cool. Uh, arc you guys staying for dinner? "Sure, we will stay," said Kevin and Veronica. We need to hang out with the grand babies for a while anyway. They went to the activity room to play with the kids while Mae and Victor got everything ready for dinner. "Hey, Aunt Mae." Victor asked: Will you please continue to stay here with us? I totally believe you and I'm glad that you were able to tell me the truth, finally. If Junise does come back, she's gonna need you to show her that she ca n beat this. "Thanks Victor," Aunt Mae said.

Just then Zandara came upstairs, "Is dinner ready yet?" "Yes, it is. Go wash up and tell Tammy and Zachary, too. Tell Nana and PopPop that dinner is ready." Okay. Zandara said, "I will". She skipped away singing, Yeah, dinner is ready, Yeah, dinner is ready!

"How or what are you gonna tell them,?" Kevin asked. "I don't know but I'm gonna tell them, Victor said. Just then Tammy asked, "Where's mom; we can't have dinner without Mom." Yes, we can and I will explain things at the table so I won't have to keep repeating it, Victor said. Everyone came together to the table. Tammy said grace and they all began eating. The kids told of their daily events and that they were excited about seeing and playing with NaNa and PopPop. They finished eating and Aunt Mae and Veronica cleared the table and cleaned everything. They got the children bathed and ready for bed. Just then, the twins said, "Storytime, Storytime"! Kevin and Veronica got ready to go. "No, don't leave yet," Victor said:" Kids, tonight I need to talk to you about something. So we won't have storytime tonight. Tammy looked at her dad and asked, "Daddy is something wrong? "Where's mommy?" Veronica quickly burst into tears. Kevin calmed her down while Victor finished talking to the children.

The children asked: Daddy, Where's mommy? She's not dead is she?" No, No, baby nothing like that! "Are you guys getting a divorce?" "No, baby, I Love Your mom, why would we get a divorce?" Well, she's not here and she's always here for storytime. Well, babies, mom's gonna be gone for a while. I have no idea how long she will be gone; but she said to let you all know that she loves you guys very much. And that she will think about you all, everyday. So, don't worry about anything, okay? "Okay," said Tammy. "Okay," said the twins.

Now, it's bedtime; tell everyone good night and I'll be back in a minute to tuck you guys in for the night. "Okay. Good night daddy, Good night Aunt Mae, Good night NaNa and PopPop," they all said together.

Wow! You handled that very well. I thought because you are so forward about Everything, you were gonna tell them the truth. "Nope, I'm not gonna destroy whatever positive image they have of their mother, Victor said. The Coopers left and Aunt Mae and Victor went to bed.

2 weeks later . . . .

The police had not found Junise; but, her car had been impounded. Detective Boone called to let Victor know that. Victor thanked him and told him he would pick the car up tomorrow.

Aunt Mae was getting the kids ready for school. Tammy asked, "when is mommy coming home? I miss her; has she even called?" "Yeah! I miss mommy too," said Zandara, "and tomorrow is her day to read to my class." Your mom is fine," Aunt Mae told the kids. Z, I will come and read to your class if your mom does not show up. Okay thanks, Aw1t Mae. Z skipped off in route to find Zach, before breakfast, so they can play checkers before school.

He was getting really good at checkers and Z was determined to beat him. Tammy was letting Aunt Mae put the finishing touches on her hair. How about, I take you guys to school today? "That will be great," Tammy said. Everything is gonna be okay, Tammy.

Your dad told you not to worry about anything, right? So don't worry. Now go upstairs and eat breakfast. Tell your brother and sister to eat, too. I will be there in twenty minutes to take you guys to school. Go enjoy your dad

I Owe You Nothing

before he goes to work. She waited for Tammy to be out of earshot. God please take care of this family. Watch over the kids and Victor. Give him the strength he needs right now, to be the parent that the kids need. Lead Him Guide Him in the right directions. And Lord, I'm asking a special blessing for my niece. Give her the strength she needs to overcome this addiction and bring her home sober, strong and complete to take care and love her family. Thank you Lord for the day and go ahead of all of us and make our day plain, smooth, and straight. I will be in continuous prayer for her. But I ask that your will be done. These and other blessings, we ask in your Precious Son, Jesus' name. Amen. Aunt Mae made it upstairs;

Victor was preparing to leave. "Have a good day, Victor." Thanks Aunt Mae, you too.

As they were driving to school, Tammy screamed, Stop The Car! Stop The Car! It's mommy! It's Mommy! Tammy, what are you talking about? Aunt Mae slowed the car down and Tammy jumped out. Tammy! Tammy! Stop! What are you doing? But, Tammy was already going toward the woman she saw and Aunt Mae stopped and parked the car. She ran after Tammy, the twins chased after Aunt Mae. Tammy, stop! We have to get you guys to school. No! I'm not.. stopping, I want mommy! Just then Tammy, stopped running. It was Junise.

Mom! Why are you not home? We miss you! Please mom come home. Just then, Tammy looked down at her mom and noticed the needle in her arm. Mom, What are you doing? Tammy started to grab the needle but Aunt Mae grabbed Tammy, just before she did. Tammy, no! The twins looked at the lady and screamed Mom!Mom! Aunt Mae grabbed them, too. She just stood there holding the kids. Junise just continued shooting and said, "Lady get these kids out of here! I don't know who their mom is but, its not me." Aunt Mae said to Junise, "you are correct! You are not these kids' mother." She lead the kids back to the car with them kicking and screaming about their mom. She was holding back tears herself. She screamed, Tammy don't you ever jump out of a moving car again! You could have been killed! "Why are you yelling at me!" Tammy belted back. Dad lied! Dad lied! "Tammy don't do this in front of Z and Zach," said

Aunt Mae. "No, you guys could have told us the truth! We are kids but we understand things, too. Mom is on drugs! She would rather do drugs than love and take care of us! Why? Why?" "Stop talking about mom like that!" Zandara screamed. "That wasn't mom!" Yeah, Zach added. She said she wasn't our mom. Tammy just stop! We are not talking about this anymore. You are going to school and I will pick you guys up later. They arrived at the school and the kids got out. Tammy stuck her head back in the car and said, "I know that was my mom", and ran into the school. Once the children were out of the car, Mae parked the car and just started to cry. Lord, what are we gonna do now?

The kids didn't need to see their mom like that. Where do we go from here".

Thanks you Lord for letting me see her.

Aunt Mae drove home and immediately called Victor to let him know what happened. "What? How could you let this happen":said Victor. Aunt Mae responded: "you can't blame me, for this. I was driving. But, Victor she looked really bad. She said that she didn't have any children. She had a needle in her arm and she didn't even know who I was. Man, I'm sorry that the children had to have that experience.

I'm gonna call Kevin and Veronica just to let them know what has happened. So at least they will know she is still alive." "Okay, I apologize, Aunt Mae. I'm just frustrated with work and these have been the worst two weeks, ever for me. I will talk to you when I get home tonight." Okay, they both hung up the phone. Aunt Mae called Kevin and Veronica and they were pleased. They stated that they would not be able to make it over that after noon.

. . . . Later that afternoon . . . .

Victor got off early. He had been going into the office early, so he could be home when the children got out of school. Aunt Mae had been in her room praying.

I Owe You Nothing

When she finished, she went into the kitchen. As she entered she saw Victor already preparing the childrens', "after school" snacks. Oh, Victor I didn't realize you had made it home, already. I guess I was praying so hard that I didn't realize the time. God is gonna get us through this. "Amen. Amen", Victor said: that is what has been carrying me through, this far. I've been listening to the Word on the radio in my office and the song, "Somebody Prayed For Me" came on and I was wondering if my wife even understands how many people are actually praying for her to get it together. Aunt Mae, I just want my life and my family back the way it was. I want to be able to talk to my wife and kids, to let them know that we shouldn't take each other for granted; that we should be able to talk as a family, and not lie to one another. "Yeah, I understand, Aunt Mae said. Well, in about 40 minutes you might have your chance because little Ms. Tammy was very upset this morning." Oh, Cindy called earlier. She stated that she and Ray would be stopping by and that they would bring Ryan and Raychelle over to play with the kids. So, I figured we could all just have a picnic in the backyard to clear our minds of the day's events. "Oh, so that explains the seasoned meat and all the tupperware in the fridge, said Victor. "Yes", said Aunt Mae. "I'm gonna make spaghetti and meatballs because I know the kids love them so much and I even baked a homemade apple pie." "Wow, well lets do it! Victor said. And I'm sure the kids will enjoy the company."

About 20 minutes later, Aw1t Mae left to go get the children. She arrived at the school and the children got in the car. The twins were bouncing around in their seats. Tammy just got in and didn't say one word all the way home. Aunt Mae turned on the radio and listened to Fred Hammond's "No Weapon," and she and the twins sang the song all the way home. When they arrived home, the twins got out of the car and went into the house, shouting: "Daddy, you're home!" They saw their snack and began eating. Tammy entered the kitchen saying, "Daddy, why did you lie to us? Mom is on drugs! You could have told us. You are a liar! I hate you!" And she ran into her room. "Tammy!" Aunt Mac started to go behind her, but Victor stopped her. "Sit here with the twins and finish what you are cooking. Tammy is my problem. So, I will go and talk to her.

She's angry with me. So I will handle it." Victor knocked on Tammy's door; "Go Away!" Tammy said. Victor went into the room and said:" Tammy, you are correct I did lie to you.

I just didn't know how to tell you, all the day that it happened. Your mother loves you. Okay? She's just going through something and apparently, drugs is her outlet. But, you do not have to worry. We have to keep living our lives and keep mommy in our prayers. God is gonna turn all this around, okay," Victor "Okay daddy, but when we saw her today and she didn't even know that we were her kids, and I saw the needle in her arm, It made me mad! How could she choose drugs over us?" Victor commented: "I don't have an answer for you sweetie. I'm sorry, but, I'm gonna need you to be the best big sister that you can, to help keep me strong and motivated. It's notgonna be easy. We just have to remember that mommy loves us, and we have Aunt Mae to help us. So, can we do this? You can't come in here mad, and slamming stuff, Okay? We are a Family; and we are not gonna let anything stop us. I Love You! I do have to tell your brother and sister the truth, though and that means you are gonna have to help me get them adjusted, too. Are you gonna be my big girl?" Yes, I Am, Tammy said. "Thanks dad. I'm sorry about all this. I'm just mad at mommy." They hugged and went downstairs. By then, Cindy and her family had arrived. They grilled and had their picnic. Itwas a great day!

2 years later . . . .

Veronica's Death:

Kevin was getting dressed. Victor, the kids and Aunt Mae arrived to ride in the family car. There were plenty of people around the house. Kevin said to Victor: "I can not believe my wife is gone. At least, we made these two years wonderful. I just wish our daughter was here. They got in the car and headed for the church. They arrived at church and the services began. Everything went well; It was a beautiful service. Zandara and Zachary sang a song and Tammy read the "Footprints" poem. Victor and Kevin were amazed at how well the children were doing. They had lost so much in these two years. As they were heading into the cemetery, Tammy looked out the car and said, "Mom!" Mae, Victor and Tammy all looked. It really was Junise. "How did she find out? What? She made it! She made it! What do you mean she made it?" I prayed for momma. That she needed to be here to say goodbye to NaNa. Aunt Mac just smiled. They made it to the grave site and they put the coffin in the ground. Aunt Mae sang the final song. After everything was over. Kevin and Victor asked Junise what she was doing there? How did she find out? She said:

"I don't know. I woke up and there was a newspaper with mom's picture on it and the information. So, I came." She looked at Victor and her kids and began to cry. "I want my family back, I want to come home; Victor, Daddy I want to kick this! I have missed so much from my kids. I've messed up my life, enough. I've put my kids through enough." Victor hugged her and said:" You can hug the kids but don't make them any promises or say anything about you coming home to them. Just, enjoy your day with them."

Later that evening, it was time to go. "Victor, can I come home, Junise asked. "No!" He said: "I have to do what's right by the kids. You just can't come off the street and expect everything to be all good. You need to go to rehab, You need parenting classes, You need to get yourself, together first. God, Aunt Mae and other people have held it together, all this time. While you have been on the streets doing, God knows what. You need to be examined for diseases. You need to learn to handle financial situations. You need to get a job and hold it down for a while. Do what you need to do for yourself, right now. You have our support.

We have always prayed that you would get it together. I understand that you just lost your mother; but my kids lost their mother over two years ago. Whenever it's time for her to come back, She has to come back correctly, or not come at all. These are the things that will make it work. Those same pressures that made you leave in the first place, are still gonna be there. They are probably gonna get a lot worse with the kids getting older and I need to know that you are strong and ready. If you come back, you are staying. You hurt me, the kids and the family. It has taken you to lose something, in order for you to even come around. I have to make sure it's not for selfish reasons. My kids will not be hurt again. Rehab, you go today.

It all ends and begins today. Basically, you have to be ready to be mom, wife and all of that when you come home. My home is a House Of God and you are not gonna disturb it again with your issues. I need a wife and the kids need a mother. If you arc gonna half—step, then we can get a divorce and it will be done."

"I totally understand," Junise said. "I'm thankful that you are willing. I felt everyone of you guys' prayers. My situation out in the streets was horrible but I know God had his hand in it because even when I was out of my mind, I would always hear Aunt Mae saying child, I'm praying for you. We all are. Then when I saw the newspaper today and I saw the back of the person as they walked away. I knew it was Aunt Mae. Thanks for everything, and yes, I'm going to rehab, parenting classes, therapy (family and personal), church and everything else, because that's what it is going to take for me to get my family back.

Junise did everything that she needed to do and her family is stronger and better than ever. She got a job at Regions Hospital and has been there for seven years and sober for eight years. As for Aunt Mae, she moved out into a one bedroom apartment, right across from the family. She still prays for them until this day.

That's why they have a lovely life together, People praying for one another. Ugly Vicious Cycles

Let's talk about this for just a bit. I know you want more scenarios but this topic is major. This is about some cycles that "donors" and "real parents" go through that might have an impact on the kids.

Kids this day and age just come out smart, and ready for what the world has to offer. But donors seem to think that they can put the real parent through whatever and it has no affect on the child. So here are some examples and how they seem to play out with the kids.

1. Taking the real parent to court—Why is this happening? Of course this happens at the donors convenience. Donors don't want the real parent and the kid to make it. They will try to stop it, at all cost. Donors don't want to pay support, and don't want to see the child/children, unless or / if they can personally benefit. The sad part is that the courts, most of the time let them not pay support or let donors pay the minimum to get it off the judges'docket. The case can be rescheduled and rescheduled and rescheduled. The real parent usually has to miss work or some major part or time in the child's life to go to court. Example: A mother has two children by a man. The first child the donor didn't really do anything for/or with the first child. But the mother keeps taking care of the child. She and the child are doing fine; they have their apartment, car and the mother is working two to three jobs just to make ends meet. All the time, the mother is longing for the donor to act responsibly, but she's called out of her name by the donor and his family. The family doesn't look down on him, or talk to him about what he is not doing for the child. Watch Out, because this is where "I Owe You Nothing" comes into play. The donor becomes homeless and has burned all his bridges with his family(yeah, the same one that talks about the mother). So, where do you think he ends up? He ends up knocking on the door of the real parent. As mad or angry as the real parent is at him, she looks at her child and thinks about her daily life; and then looks at her child's face and how happy that child is to even see the donor. It is difficult for her to see the donor as a homeless man. She gives in and lets him move into their apartment, thinking that she is given her child the father and family that her child dese1-ves. The question is: Should she have done this or let him figure it out for himself? The answer is: Lock The Dam Door and Let Him Knock! The reason is: As the real parent, you end up being the one doing all the trying to make things work. Back to the story, they end up living together and the mother realizes she's pregnant, again. She tells him that he can leave now because she's pregnant and she does not want him to leave, once times get hard. However, because he still needs a place to live, he promises her that he's gonna stay and they are gonna be the perfect family. But, i n his head, he thinks: oh she's pregnant, again. She's not going anywhere, anyways. Arguments start that were not started before. They begin having little fights that were not going on before. So, eventually, the mother gets tired because now they are fighting in front

of the first child. Therefore, she puts the man out for her safety and the safety of the child. She files a restraining order; of course, he contests it. They go to court and the judge dismisses or refuses the restraining order. Eventually, the second baby is born and the father is mad about child support. The mother gets papers saying that, she needs to be in court. She goes to court and the judge asks her, what would be a fair amount because the donor has other obligations. She gives the judge the amount and the donor surprisingly says he wants joint custody of the kids.

However, he never pays child support or pays less than the $50 dollar minimum. Therefore, they have to go to family court. More court dates are being rescheduled, etc. Family court time finally comes and guess what happens? The man doesn't have to pay anymore child support and the Judge states that he is to get the children every two weeks and the mom has to provide clothing, accessories and toys for the children. The mother explains to the judge that it's not fair that she has to supply everything, just because she makes more money than the donor. The mother always has to provide for the kids. All that the donor ever does, is barely take care of himself. He never buys clothes, food or anything to help, when the mother has the kids. But now she has to supply for the kids, when they are with the donor, as well. So the date and time is set for pickups and drop-offs. They agree, he will pick the kids up from their maternal grandmother's on Friday at 6:00pm. The first weekend, he shows up at 6:30p.m. The n '1 time he's suppose to get the kids he picks them up at 6:40p.m. not ever calling to say that he's gonna be late, even though, this is what he is court—ordered to do. The kids' birthday weekends come and he was suppose to have them that weekend. But then, he calls the mother about switching weekends, because its their birthdays. Basically, he is saying that he didn't want to have to spend money for their birthdays. Then, he just stopped coming to get the kids, stopped calling, and stopped all communications. This is where the cycle comes into effect, The kids want to see their donor, but all, that the mom can tell the kids is that they can not go because she does not know how to get in contact with the donor. Now, the mom is the mean one because she has to hear her children cry and even have fits, because they can't see the donor anymore. The donor hates the mom now, so, he doesn't want to see the kids, eventhough, it has been court ordered. The mom did what the judge ordered her to do.

The mom even wrote the judge; because she's not able to just contact the judge by phone. Of course, the clerk said something about doing an amendment to the order to get the donor to follow the order or suffer the consequences.

But, of course, that costs money. So, since the mom only owes her kids, and owes nothing to the donor, she just gives the whole situation to God. She owes it to herself to be stress free. She considers it to be his lost. You would wonder: a) Would he ever start seeing the kids again? b) Will the kids adapt to not seeing the donor? c) Will the tears ever end? d) Will the donor even try to explain things to the kids if he gets to see them again? Or will he just blame the mother? e) Why does he not want to be involved with his children?

These are just a few questions that probably went through the mother's head.

Example Two: The egg donor(mother) who gives everything (especially her kids) up, for her man. She's always leaving the kids with whomever she can; because the man that she loves or wants to be with doesn't want anything to do with her children. So, the children are attached to everyone else who keeps them or who spends time with them. They have no respect for their mother, at all. They won't listen to her. They never want to go home, with her, in fear that the mother's boyfriend will come and they will have to be watched by someone else. They may fear that the mother will put them to sleep depending on the age of the oldest one, so that she can go and do whatever she desires with her man. The children are practically, raising themselves. The mother never helps the children with homework; her man is dressed; drives a new car that the kids can not even sit in, less thought of riding in it. However, this egg donor is spending whatever money she has on the man that she is with.

Let's see the cycle: a) The children will probably not learn how to be mothers or fathers unless some of the other people step up and show them the right way. b) The children will probably end up being bad parents or donors themselves. c) She is possibly teaching her daughters that its okay to take care of a man and teaching her sons that its okay to be taken care of; instead of teaching them that hardwork is its own reward; and that, if you don't take care of yourself or each other(spouse) that you will end up with nothing. d) You have to teach your kids, so that they will teach your grandkids.

Example Three: This is gonna make a whole lot of people mad. This cycle is called the absent parent cycle. My mom or dad was not there, for me. So, I'm not gonna be there for my children. Now this vicious cycle has to stop somewhere. Why not let it stop with you. Now if one or maybe both of your parents were not there for you, You should want to be with your kids. No one should have to beg you or talk about you in order for this to be done; it's something you should want to do. Even, if you are not with the real parent, you should still be there in that child's face, often. It might be hard to do everyday (depending on your situation or availability). But, if you are a donor and not working then it should be everyday. Don't punish the child because you and the real parent don't get along or because your parent wasn't there for you. Case and point: Remember I Owe You Nothing.

A man has four children with four different women. His father was not present at all in his life. He was raised by his mother and her new husband, who was abusive to the young man and his sisters, as kids. When the man had his kids, guess what? He has not stepped up to the plate for any of the kids for the most part. His mother and sisters help with the kids, when they come over to visit. The only reason he participates with the last two kids is because he can stay in between the two moms because they provide a place for him to live. But, the kids hardly even see each other and the two mothers are mad at everyone but him. He doesn't see the second child at all; and the mom won't even let the donor's family see the child, either. When the oldest child does visit the mother and sister, the donor won't even attempt to see the child. The child is practically a teenager. He longs for the donor and the donor's attention. The donor does not work because of felonies, even though, the state/city in which the donor lives has felony friendly jobs available. He fears he won't have any money, or enough money, so he chooses not to get involved or get a job. Shoot, he can get two felony friendly jobs if that's the case. The state in which he lives can only take child support from one job. He acts like the kids owe him something. (i.e. they are suppose to just want to see him). He acts like the children just suppose to jump into his arms. This statement applies for egg donors, too. The children don't owe donors, an explanation about anything. Donors owe the children an CA1Jlanation. You should want to be better parents, if your parents were not around for you. You should want your children to see that they are important to you and that they are not burdens. You know what you went through without that parent being there. Why would you want to put your child through that?

They deserve you! They don't owe you! Stop blaming them for your laziness! If you eat, your kids should eat! Hell, if you don't eat, your kids should eat!

Sometimes that is a sacrifice a real parent would make. The cycle must stop. That's why the kids these days are lost. The parents didn't have parents so then they kept the cycle going, by not being there for their children. a) Who does this cycle hurt in th e end? b) Will the cycle ever stop? c) How vicious is this particular cycle?

These are just a few cycles to put on your mind. These are questions that you might ask yourself, if you are a donor, as well, as if you are a real parent. Usually, you know about your donors past or childhood. You know if their parents were involved with them. You can try your best to instill in them not to be bad parents. Instill in them to turn that negative absence into a positive presence for their children. Let them know you and the children need them to help instill in the children, good morals and values in life and work.

I'd Rather Do Time, Than Pay For What's Mine

This part of the book is dedicated to the donors that would rather go to jail than pay child support or take care of the blessing that God has given to them. why on God's beautiful earth would you rather sit amongst non— productive individuals (prostitutes, drug dealers, murderers, rapist), than to have your freedom and the love of your child. This is not just about the donors who don't have the time and money. What about the ones that have the money and still don't pay or spend time with the children. Guess what? The child is still missing out. Can you imagine the jail house conversation? It might go a little something like(Forgive me for not knov.ing the lingo) but, here it goes: 'What are you in for? I'm here for raping someone. And you? I'm here for not paying child support. 'What? That's it? Are you crazy? You can be out there free to see your kids, love them freely and you are stuck in here. (Does anyone else feel like there should be a bitch slap right here)? Oh, back on focal point. Don't you know there are people in this place that would kill just to have half of what you got going? They would love: to be able to do things with their children; and buy their children the things they need, and some of the things they might want. You are getting a record so that even now, you probably won't be able to get employment. You just mad e the situation more difficult to spend time with them. Do you a ctually think that the real parent will bring that child to visit you while you are sitting there? You are taking the risk of becoming someone's jail house whore rather, than to step up and be responsible. well, this episode should get you the respect you need in here.

Hey, let's make a pact. If anyone else asks you why you are here, here's a tip: Tell them you are a murderer. 'Why a murderer? First of all because i t sounds better. Secondly, you are killing yourself and your child's dreams of being loved and taken care of by both parents. You are killing yourself and your child's relationship. I know, you probably think that you are hurting the real parent. 'Who is free and out there with the child. But thats it, the real parent is free and able to do anything they want to do and now because you are in the system. You now are limited to do. Not only do for yourself but your child also. But let's see what the donors excuse or acceptance of what has taken place.

Well, I'm in here, and out there, I didn't have what I needed. Now I have three hots and a cot, television, and computers. The taxpayers are now taking care of me even, better than I was myself. The child will get over it. And even if the child doesn't, who cares? I'm good!

See, the other inmate slates: That's what I'm talking about. You are grown and feel like the taxpayers are helping you out. But, your child is out there with one parent that is doing everything in their power to take care of that child, You on the other hand, are sitting in here being selfish and ignorant.

Let me tell you a story. See, I've personally been in the system for many years. I've seen and heard a lot of things. But this story, I'm gonna tell you hopefully will change your outlook on your situation.

There was a man named Julian Tarver. Julian was a hardworking manager at a local coffee shop. Everyday, he would see this one beautiful lady named Shauni. They would flirt back and forth until one day Julian got brave enough to ask Shauni out on a date. They began dating exclusively.

Shauni was a state employee. She was the database manager for the state. She handled the computer problems of the state employees. But, her vice was she needed coffee. They dated for about six months and then their relationship became sexual. Well, one night they had sex with no protection, just spontaneously. Three months later, Shauni discovers she's pregnant. She tells Julian.

The first thing he says of course, the baby is not mine. Shauni is furious, she tried everything in her power to prove it to him. That March, Eric Julian Tarver was born into the world. Shauni was so happy. She was a great mother to Eric.

She would still go into the coffee shop and get her coffee and would see Julian there, everyday. They never exchanged words or anything. Eric would be with his mom because he attended the daycare that was in her building.

So one day out of spite, Julian decided to go to the county and asked for a paternity test. Shauni and Eric went and had the testing done. Julian of course, went and had his done with the cockiness, saying: "the whole time that baby ain't mine." He started calling Shauni, calling her a whore and saying that he wasn't the dad and just leaving harassing messages. Shauni being the woman she was, stopped answering the phone and let the answering machine get everyone of those harassing messages from Julian. Six weeks later, the results are in: In the case of Eric Julian Tarver, Julian you are the father (Sorry I had to throw a Maury moment in there). by the probability of 99.999 percent!

So, the county began their paperwork and Julian signed the "Recognition of Parentage and became the legal father for Eric. Well, because he had this done, Shauni had a spiteful moment, too. So, she asked for child support. This of course, made Julian outrage! You know, I only make enough money to take care of myself! Why would you put me on child support? Shauni responded: "You arc the Father 99•999 percent", and she left it at that.

Two months later, their case had made it to court. The judge heard the arguments and asked for their information about where they worked.

Julian tried to say he didn't make much money and the judge asked him how much he made per hour. He stated he was just a regular employee and that he only made six dollars an hour. Shauni objected and told the judge everything.

She even had an old checkstub of his and said this is how much he made, before Eric was born.

He's the manager. When I go in there for my coffee, everyday, I have a camera phone and I take pictures of him working. "Let me see", said the judge. She showed the pictures to the judge, the paystub showing him making thirteen dollars an hour, and the pictures showed that he was the manager. The judge was furious!

"Mr. Tarver, do you know that I could have you arrested for lying to me?! This is a serious matter! There is an innocent child involved." Now, let's see here. The judge asked if he had other kids or obligations; and he said: "No

I Owe You Nothing

Your Honor", He's the only one. The judge made her decision. Mr. Tarver and Ms. Scott this is my ruling: Mr. Tarver will pay$ 375.00 a month for child support. He will also pay one-half of the child's medical/dental expenses, with a fifty dollar increase every two years, until the child turns five years old. I will then make other adjustments at that time. This order starts now. And if you miss more than three payments Mr. Tarver you are going to jail for non payment of child support. You must also keep your job. The moment you don't work, you will be locked up. Yeah, judge, you better say that," Julian said.

I am gonna quit tomorrow; so you might as well lock me up, today. Because, I Would Rather Do The Time, Than Take Care of what's Mine! "Mr. Tarver, I'm warning you!" "Lock me up your Honor", Julian said. Shauni was shocked! She couldn't do or say anything. How could a man be so cold about taking care of someone, so innocent? How could he be so selfish? The inmate paused, for a minute, while the donor inmate begged him to finish the story. Okay, here we go: Julian was placed under arrest for contempt of court and for refusing to pay child support. The judge gave him the maximum sentence five years because of his actions and his refusal. "Wow" said the donor inmate; five years, that's a lot!

"Oh, I'm not done," stated the older inmate, there's more to the story." You have got to be kidding," said the donor inmate. "No I'm not," said the older inmate.

Well, Julian went into prison a man, but as soon as the inmates discovered the real reason he was there, Julian's life became a living hell. He thought the same way you do, three hots and a cot. He was raped every night and his cellmate, Big Bernard raped him, too. Bernard told him it was because he didn't have a father in his life. So, he was gonna be Julian's punisher. Well, one night Mr. Julian waited until Big Bernard was done raping him and had fallen asleep. Julian then pulled out a butcher's knife that he had stolen from the kitchen.

He took that knife and killed Big Bernard. The next day, as they opened the cell, Big Bernard's body was found and Julian was standing there holding the knife in his hand with Bernard's blood dripping from the knife. The guards immediately, hand cuffed Julian. A few weeks later, Julian was charged with Big Bernard's death. He had pleaded guilty. The judge told him twenty-five years and then he would be put to death by lethal injection. Julian was furious! So, almost everyday he would be in some sort of fight and end up in the hole to avoid being raped and from any retaliation from Big Bernard's friends.

Years passed and eventually all of Big Bernard's friends had either passed away or had been released. So, Julian felt it was safe to just be a prisoner; it was for a while, but, then Julian got into a fight that added another six months to his sentence.

. . . . 25 years later . . . .

A news reporter enters the prison to interview the man who killed the biggest drug dealer in Alabama. The reporter enters and Julian is escorted into the room. He introduced himself as Eric. "Really?" Julian said and just let out a hmph!" That's a coincidence", Eric said." excuse me?' replied Eric. "Oh, nothing", said Julian; I'm just thinking to myself. "Is it okay if l record this interview," Eric asked. "I will be coming here all week to talk with you." "Sure, that's fine," said Julian.

The Interview Begins:

Eric: I guess the first question would be how and why did you kill Big Bernard Powell?

Julian: I killed him with a butcher's knife that I had stolen from the kitchen since that was the duty that I had at the time; working in the kitchen.

Julian: Why did I kill him? He was my cellmate and he raped me, every night.

A man can only toke so much.

Eric: Did you ask why he was raping you?

I Owe You Nothing

Julian: Yes, he said he was punishing me, for rather coming to jail than to take care of my son. He was upset because his father was absent in his life. Eric: While you were being raped or even after being raped ; did you think that the child that you chose not to take care of; would probably end up as mean or bad as Bernard?

Julian: No, I hadn't given that a thought at all.

Eric: Okay, well I think that's enough for today. We will end this part of the interview for the day. if I need anything else, I will ask tomorrow or later on in the week.

Eric: Have a good rest of your day, Mr. Tarver. Julian: You too Eric.

Eric came back to continue his interview everyday that week. They talked about everything, including the fact that Julian would be getting the lethal injection in a few months. Finally, Friday came and Eric asked Julian if he had any regrets about the choices he had made.

Julian: "Yes". I wish I could meet my son, just to see how he turned out.

I pray that he is not in the system or anything like that, and if I could just meet him and see him before I get my injection, I could die a happy man. Eric: Well, did you keep in contact with his mother at all?

Julian: Well, that's funny because Shauni use to write all the time, but she never would send a picture of our son. She wrote up until about two years ago. Site would just write a bunch of prayers for me.

In the last letter that she wrote she did. finally say something about our child. She said that he turned out to be a great man and an excellent father to his twins.

She wrote that he named them (Eric.finished Julian's statement).

Eric: Julian and Juliana.

Julian: How did you know that Eric? Did you meet her before and interview her? "No". Eric said.

Eric: "I've known her all my life. She was my mother. What do you mean was?

Well my mom died two years ago. She told me that she had written you a letter.

A week after writing it, she died. well, I guess you got what you wanted, Mr. Tarver. You got to see me before you could get your injection. You got what you wanted, but I never got what I needed: A relationship with you. The reason I gave my kids their names is to remind me to always be a Father, first. So, now you can die happy. Julian: Son, I'm sorry.

Eric: Mr. Tarver, I told you to call me Eric. "You don't have a son." Eric got up and left. The next day Eric's story came out in the paper. The headline read: Finally Got To Meet My Dad! "The Man Who Killed Big Bernard Powell". But guess who did not get to read the paper, Julian. He died in his sleep that night. He never even made it to the lethal injection. "The guilt must have killed him," Eric said, when he was informed about Julian's death.

See, said the older inmate. The same people you meet going up are the same people you meet going down. You have no idea who or what you will come across in your lifetime. It Might Be The Child You Refused To Take Care Of!

. . . . Taking Care of What You Are Blessed With . . . .

This part of the book is for the real parents who are taking care of their blessings that they were given. I am so proud of you all. Congratulations! You love the person and your child/children enough to stay, to go through everything and the everyday situations. You don't have to depend on one person, you have each other to depend on, Possibly, two incomes or even, if one doesn't work, there's still support there on some level.

It has taken me a while to write this part of the book because I find it difficult to write about. You bind together to make your family work. There are people from teenage to adulthood, who dream or try to make the situation work where both parents are involved in the child's life.

They dream of the day their donor will get it right and not be selfish. In your being responsible pa rents working together, I pray that it will show someone that if they can do it, so can I. The parent and donor can see that I can love my child, and the other parent. I can stick through hard times and baby cries.

I can take ca re of the blessing that I am given. r will say this: don't just stay together because of the kids unless you are gonna express love, all the time. Not saying there will not be arguments or anything like that, but show them that through God or whatever your Higher Power may he love and sacrifice all these things are possible. So keep doing what you are doing and continue to take care and love what you are blessed with.

. . . . Don't Turn A Willing Parent Into A Donor . . .

If a parent is willing to be a parent, allow them to be a parent, whether you all are together or not. Don't be an idiot! Don't turn them into a donor.

Accept the positive things that they have to offer the child. Let them do for the child. If the other parent is willing to buy pampers, food, clothes or whatever, let them. Don't punish the child. If that parent is willing to come visit with the child(especially if you all are not a couple), the child needs and deserves to have two willing parents in their lives. The willing parent is putting forth the efforts to not be a donor. So as the main parent, help them. That does not mean sucker them for their money. Accept the clothes or whatever. Be thankful! Be thankful! Willing Parents, make sure you keep your receipts. You never know when the situation might change. You might need them, as proof one day.

You are showing your child that they are loved by both parents. Even if the willing parent is not there. The child will at least learn tolerance, respect and know love. The willing parent should never feel like giving up, because the other parent does not know how to accept positive things. Willing parents don't let them take you there. Keep your focus on your child, not on the other parent. Keep doing the right thing. Kill donors with kindness. And always take care of what's yours. If you ever feel like not trying or becoming a donor, look into or imagine your child's face, when he/she sees you, or the things that you are doing for them.

Remember that moment of being. Proud of you being a parent. Know your rights! Your child is at least worth that. Don't just take the other parents words of what they are gonna do for you. There are rights out their for you. Legal Aide is available.

I know real parents there are some things that I missed; I apologize. I just want to get some of the main things on some general subjects. But, I want this to be an eye—opener to donors and to young people or even older people that are embarking on being on becoming parents. That before a decision is made that someone in the relationship/sex buddy scenario might have read this book and open up these as well as any other discussion that they might arise and it will help them make a more positive decision or teach others how to react if they are currently in any of these situations. They will learn or know that Kids Come First and how to handle themselves as parents and might help the don ors realize how to become a real parent. Parenting is Universal. It's not a black, white, brown, yellow or whatever thing. Its A Universal I Want to Be A Real Parent Thing! Its a Kid Thing! And They Owe You Nothing!

I Know I Was Adopted

(told by Jairus)

I was told this story by one of the greatest storytellers there will ever be. My handsome oldest son Jairus. See this is why I Owe You Nothing is so important to me. You never know what you or who you are raising. Or what the impact of what you instill in them will come out of them.

The story starts with us sitting out on the porch of a townhouse we lived in. Jairus said, "Mom you arc the best mom ever". But I know I was adopted.

I asked, "Jairus why would you say that; you were not adopted". "Uh huh" he said. I was adopted because I was in Heaven with God and he placed me in your stomach and gave me to you. So I came out of your stomach so I was adopted by you. But I came from God. I had always been so proud of Jairus but when he told me this I cried. Because it showed me that I was doing a good job as a person and it showed me that I was taken very good care of what God had blessed me with. For me it was confirmation that me taking my kids to church and that out of the mouths of babes the words can truly stick to you. Here I was in one of my dark moments and my 5 year old brought joy and sunshine to my life in that instant. To let me know that God loved us enough to give us blessings and let us adopt the lives he has made. Thanks for the story and being such a loving child Jairus. Jairus tells all types of stories and maybe in other books i will share them with you. I wonder what Jaiden will come up with soon. I Love My Babies!

I Owe You Nothing

(Acknowledgments)

First, I want to thank God for giving me the vision and ability to write. I want to thank my children: Jairus and Jaiden; my mother Betty, my dad Victor (r.i.p) my dad Otto. I want to thank my sisters:

Katina, Tammy, Iesha, Tiesha, Dineen, my bestie Debbie, Z, Kendra, Kate and any other sister of mine that have touched me in my life. If I forgot to mention you, I totally apologize; Charge it to my head and not my heart. I want to thank my brothers, Michael, Victor, Marquise, Tarrie, Freddie and Fredrick, and Charles Thanks to my nieces and nephews: Katia, Chevella, D'Myshea, Kevosier, Tyvarres and Tyrelle also their brothers and sisters and cousins as well.

You are all a part of my family. To my extended family, I love You all. You have All inspired me in your own way. You all know, once you are in the family, you Are in the family. Thanks goes out to Bigman, to my daughters, Jessica(chuckie), Precious, and Angelique(moochie) Hudson, Mrs. Barb, sperm and egg donors, real parents, single parents, married parents, donor families, and court systems. I want to send a special thank you to my fellow co-workers who dealt with me during my time of writing. You have all helped me in ways that you could not even imagine. ES baby, ES! Regions Reprocessing Department, thank you. To anyone that I have ever worked with and had to deal with me and my issues. God Bless You All! I want to thank my aunts, uncles, all my cousins especially the ones I grew up with (Dream Team Scientist). Lol. A special thank you to Alfred(kiki) and Wil. I will always love you two. Thanks for always staying in touch with me.

To all my loves that I have loved and lost thank you all too. I didn't burn the bridge so lets always keep those lines of communications open. To all my friends, God—parents of me and my kids, God brothers and sisters and my angels that walk around daily. Special thanks Gabby, Justin, Sou a, Lis, Scott, Betty Ann, Soua, Tee, Kao, Steve X, Steve J, Kieth W, The Hardimans, Stephan K, Duane K, Cardi, Joeleen, Kayla, Reese, Cassie, Lashea, Abuwi, Jason, Lee, Maurice, Steve G, AndreS, Duane K, Felicia T, Roly Poly crew, my brother in law, Cummings family of Ohio, Class of 1993 EHS, my Louisana family, my Arkansas family, my Missouri family, Arthur Jr., my Phoenix family, my Minnesota family and my church family.

The Hillers, Robert Scott, Cousin Nip, Patricia and Shirley, The Johnson Sharpe family, Black, Mr. Craig K., the Texas Crew, Amanda and Antonio, The Manley family and my homie John Boy Owens. God has blessed me with all of you for a reason. I just pray that it has not all been seasonal. Each of you have inspired me as well. God Bless You All. I Love You All So Much.

A special thanks to Mrs. Willarene Beasley my editor and church angel, thank you for the extra motivation and for keeping me on track so I was able to get my message out and educate people on the growing problem of donors. I have been wanting to write books for years. So, I said that "no matter what, I needed to focus and get started." So, here it is and I hope you all enjoy. Thank you so much for taking the time to read about things that are important and close to me. Hopefully, it will be the first of many.

To all of my new found fans, I pray that you all enjoy this book and I pray that it will touch your lives in a positive way. I pray new love for donors and kids.

I pray for prevention and that conversations can be opened between teenagers and parents, adults and their partners or even teenagers in the midst of making that big decision. Hopefully, this book will help them look at the big picture before taking a big step. I can only pray that this book helps in some way

Thanks for taking the time to purchase and read my first book. Enjoy with much love and I can only pray that people will know that Kids Come First! And Enjoy I Owe You Nothing! God Bless!

About The Author

Victoria is a mother of two handsome boys ages, nine and five. She was born in Lake Village, Arkansas, and grew up in a town called Eudora, Arkansas. Victoria graduated from Eudora High School in 1993. She also studied a semester at Philander Smith College in Little Rock, Arkansas. She later attended Lakeland Medical Dental Academy where she received a certificate as a Medical Assistant. She traveled many places in the U.S.A.; and has spent a full life. She is a hard-worker, dedicated mother to her children, and an all around good friend. She loves to write, read, cook and hangout with people. She also loves to plan parties. But most of all she loves to sec parents and their interactions with their children.

She currently lives in Saint Paul, Minnesota where she and her two boys Reside with her parents while she is in recovery from multiple strokes and seizures.

She enjoys her children, she loves God and currently attends church at the Mount Olivet Missionary Baptist Church where she participates in the greeters ministry. She hopes in the future that she will be able to continue to write books that people will love and will have some positive effect in others' lives.

She prays that her children will become great men in the world.

This book is dedicated to Amanda and Antonio. The situation, it will get greater, later. God Bless You!

Turning negative options into positive outcomes.

www.ingramcontent.com/pod-product-compliance
Lightning Source LLC
LaVergne TN
LVHW091602060526
838200LV00036B/961